THE 9 X 13 PAN COOKBOOK

Barbara Karoff

Bristol Publishing Enterprises
San Leandro, California

A Nitty Gritty® Cookbook

Printed in the United States of America.

ISBN 1-55867-031-9

Library of Congress Catalog Card Number 91-075894

Cover design: Frank Paredes
Front cover photography: Kathryn Opp
Back cover photography: Linda Sue Scott
Illustrator: Kathleen Patterson-Estes

CONTENTS

For my Mother, Bobbie and Linda.

To my generous and talented friends
Dale Barnecott, Nan Dowd, Mary Lynn Dundas,
Joyce Dutton, Nancy Gerst, Ann Henderson,
Rita Kramer, Phyllis Lindsay, Jo Miller,
Marty Sherman, Phyllis Soave and Rose Marie Weil,
thank you.

INTRODUCTION

This is a book of recipes for the 9-inch by 13-inch pan. At a time when pan sizes are as variable as almost everything else in our lives, the familiar 9 x 13 remains readily available, its time-tested usefulness undiminished.

The most important reason this venerable pan is so securely entrenched in our kitchens is that it really *is* useful, a first choice piece of equipment for cooking and serving dishes that span our menus from appetizers to desserts.

Large families have long depended on several of these practical pans to see them through meal preparation and serving. For today's relaxed entertaining style, what better dish to present the best company fare for a party or buffet? For potlucks, church socials, informal meetings or picnics, the 9 x 13 pan is ready for service. Plan-ahead meals are easy with a 9 x 13 pan. Make a dish, refrigerate or freeze it, and it's ready when you are. Creative cooks are especially attracted to recipes for a 9 x 13 pan because many of them can be easily changed, varied, or adapted to suit particular needs or preferences.

These pans, generically designated by their size, are available in styles that range from completely utilitarian to fit-for-a-party fancy. The materials from which they are made range from basic metal to the finest porcelain — with price differences that are comparable.

Capacity

If you are adapting recipes from your files to use in a 9 x 13 pan, two things should be kept in mind. The first is capacity. Three quarts or 12 cups fill the 9 x 13 pan. This is approximately double the volume of an 8 x 8 pan, should you choose to double a recipe designed for the smaller pan. A 10 x 6 pan equals 1½ quarts or 6 cups, exactly half the capacity of a 9 x 13 pan. An 11 x 7 pan equals 2 quarts or 8 cups.

Many round casserole dishes come in 1, 1½, 2, 2½, and 3 quart sizes. Most of these are deeper than the 9 x 13 pan and that is the second point to keep in mind. If recipes are adapted to our pan, watch carefully the first time you use them to correct the baking time, which will probably be less, because the food will be spread more thinly in the shallow pan.

From refrigerator or freezer to oven

If a dish requiring baking has been prepared ahead in a 9 x 13 pan and refrigerated or frozen, it needs only to be brought to room temperature and popped into the oven. There are on the market special pans designed to go from the freezer to the oven. If you own that type, they save time.

Any dish prepared for the freezer must be well and properly packaged. Wrap the dish air-tight in freezer wrap or heavy duty foil and freeze it quickly in the coldest part of the freezer. Plan to use it within a few weeks.

Covers

Most 9 x 13 pans don't come with covers, but a number of the recipes included in this collection call for covered baking. Unless you happen to have a cover that does double duty on your 9 x 13 pan, use heavy duty foil. It can be "custom-fitted" to cover the pan as loosely or as tightly as required.

Traveling with cooked food in the pan

If you carry food in the pan to another location, wrap it well in heavy duty foil and, if it is still hot or warm and you want to keep it that way, wrap it again in several thicknesses of newspaper. When you arrive at your destination, keep the dish warm (without the newspapers) in a 200° oven.

Hints and tips

- A 3½ pound chicken yields about 3 cups of cooked meat. Two whole chicken breasts equal about 1½ cups.

- One quarter pound of cheese (4 ounces) becomes 1 cup, grated.

- A number of recipes call for dry white wine. My solution to having that ingredient on hand is to purchase a large bottle of dry vermouth. No refrigeration is required and it does not turn to vinegar — ever. If you choose not to use an alcoholic ingredient, substitute fruit juices, stock, or water.

- A few recipes require that you flatten chicken or other pieces of meat, or that you pound them to uniform thickness. This is an important step which allows the meat to cook evenly. A mallet designed especially for this purpose is essential and several varieties are marketed at kitchen specialty stores. Be sure *not* to use one with a serrated or sharply pointed end. These tools are intended to tenderize tough cuts of meat and will destroy the more tender ones. Always place the pieces of meat to be flattened between two sheets of waxed paper before pounding, and pound carefully. Very little pressure is needed.

Ingredients

A few words about ingredients. I'll start with olives, about which I feel strongly. Canned California black olives of standard size, shape, and taste are available pitted, whole, sliced, or chopped. They are convenient and they add what they add to a recipe. If, however, you can locate the much more interesting varieties from Mediterranean countries, try substituting them in a favorite recipe that calls for olives and see what a difference they make. Large Kalamata olives from Greece, tiny Nicoise olives from France and the many brine or dry-cured varieties from Italy and Spain are available canned or at specialty shops and delicatessens. I've yet to find any pitted for our convenience, but especially the softer varieties release their seeds easily when pressed on a board or plate with your thumb. It's an added step, and a somewhat messy one, but these olives provide an extraordinary flavor difference.

I'm also completely in favor of using only the best cheeses. Of course, the rule about quality applies not only to cheese, but to all ingredients. Any dish is only as good as what goes into it. I've tried to use as few canned and prepared products as possible although certain dishes do not suffer from their inclusion.

Many recipes call for canned tomato sauce, a convenience item that is difficult to fault. A good homemade variety, however, will add its special flavor to any dish.

Canned beans save time and are fine in most recipes.

Canned tomatoes are often preferable to out of season "fresh ripe" ones but if in-season fresh ripe ones are available, by all means use them. In cooked dishes, peel and seed tomatoes. Otherwise the skins come off and curl up unattractively and the seeds tend to be bitter. Tomatoes (and peaches, too) peel easily after a quick dip in boiling water. To remove seeds, cut tomatoes in half and squeeze gently.

Canned corn is acceptable, but frozen corn is fresher tasting. Canned peas are not acceptable. Frozen ones are fine but must be added at the last minute to retain their fresh taste. Chopped frozen onions are a time-saver I cannot fault.

If available, fresh herbs are preferable to dried. They are not as potent, so use twice as much. Italian flat-leaf parsley packs a lot more flavor than the more common curly variety.

Do not wash fresh mushrooms. Brush them with a mushroom brush (a gadget that really works) or with a damp towel. They absorb too much water if washed.

Because personal tastes and requirements differ, most of my recipes do not list specific measure for salt and pepper. Chili powder and curry powder are also subject to personal preference. Always taste and then correct the seasonings in any recipe.

Finally . . .

This collection includes a number of recipes that have come from dear friends of long standing and are for dishes I have enjoyed at their tables over the years. Others I have chosen from my files; they represent dishes I have successfully made and served since I first began cooking.

Many of the special tips and suggestions included with particular recipes are ingredient "updates." I live in the birthplace of California cuisine, and its exuberance and allegiance to freshness have influenced and changed the way I cook. For me, California cuisine means two things: the freshest possible ingredients and innovation.

If, in working with my old recipes, I found I could successfully update them by including different or more provocative flavor combinations, I have done so, and I add a challenge to the cook to not only try my suggestions but to come up with others as well.

My advice, now as always, is to think creatively. Let a printed recipe be a guide, not a master. Recipes for a 9 x 13 pan are a perfect place to experiment — and enjoy.

BREAKFAST AND BRUNCH

MARTY'S BREAKFAST BAKE

Servings: 10-12

This is a brunch favorite of which there are many variations. Served with a hearty green salad and a light dessert, it is also perfect for lunch or supper.

slices of bread to cover a 9 x 13 pan, about 6-8
butter or margarine
1½ lbs. sweet Italian or country pork sausage, cut up
2 cups thinly sliced onions
2 cups thinly sliced mushrooms

1 lb. grated sharp cheddar cheese
5 eggs, beaten
2½ cups milk
3 tbs. Dijon mustard
1 tsp. grated nutmeg
2 tbs. chopped parsley

Butter bread slices and arrange them in the bottom of a 9 x 13 pan. Sauté sausage and onions until meat is cooked. Add mushrooms and cook 3 to 4 minutes more. Drain off excess fat and spoon mixture over bread. Top with grated cheese. Combine eggs, milk, mustard, nutmeg and parsley; pour over cheese.

Cover and refrigerate overnight or up to 24 hours. Let stand at room temperature for 30 minutes and then bake at 350° for 1 hour. Let stand for 5 minutes before serving. Cut into squares to serve.

BREAKFAST EGGS FOR A CROWD

Servings: 8-10

Here's another convenient breakfast dish that can and should be prepared the night before. For calorie watchers, use 2 (8 oz.) packages of egg substitutes.

2 tbs. butter or margarine, melted
12 eggs, scrambled "runny"
1/4 cup chopped green onions

2 cups chopped ham or Canadian bacon
1 cup sliced mushrooms

Sauce

2 tbs. butter or margarine
2 tbs. flour

2 cups milk
1 cup grated sharp cheddar cheese

Topping

1/4 cup butter or margarine, melted

13/4 cups dry bread crumbs

Combine 2 tbs. melted butter, scrambled eggs, green onions, ham and mushrooms and spoon mixture into a 9 x 13 pan. In a saucepan melt 2 tbs. butter. Stir in flour and gradually whisk in milk. Stir over low heat until sauce begins to thicken. Stir in cheese and cook until cheese is melted. Pour sauce over eggs. Combine 1/4 cup melted butter with crumbs and sprinkle over top. Refrigerate covered overnight. Let stand at room temperature for 30 minutes and then bake at 350° for 30 minutes. Cut into squares to serve.

BAKED CHEESE SANDWICHES

Servings: 10-12

This filling dish is also perfect for a cold winter evening. It tastes almost like cheese fondue, and is ready in a matter of minutes.

slices of firm white bread to cover a 9 x 13 pan, about 6 to 8
¾ cup dry white wine
½ tsp. grated nutmeg
2 eggs, well beaten
2 cups grated Swiss cheese
3 tbs. butter or margarine

Place bread slices in a lightly buttered 9 x 13 pan to cover the bottom. Spoon wine over bread; allow it to soak in. Add nutmeg and cheese to beaten eggs and blend well. Spread over bread. Dot with butter and bake at 350° for 10 to 15 minutes or until cheese is golden and bubbly. Cool 5 minutes before serving.

BAKED FRENCH TOAST SUPREME

Servings: 6-8

The better the bread, the better this dish. If you can get a good bakery loaf and cut it into extra thick slices (about 1 inch), you will be rewarded. This dish makes a breakfast or brunch into an occasion.

14 slices cinnamon-raisin bread
½ cup unsalted butter or margarine, melted
4 whole eggs
2 egg yolks
¾ cup sugar

3 cups milk and 1 cup heavy cream or 4 cups half and half
1 tbs. vanilla
powdered sugar
3 cups fresh berries or 3 cups other fresh fruit, cut up

Brush both sides of bread with melted butter and arrange slices evenly in the bottom of a buttered 9 x 13 pan. In a large bowl, beat together whole eggs and egg yolks. Beat in milk, cream and vanilla. Strain this custard over bread, making sure that each slice is evenly moistened.

Bake at 350° for 25 minutes or until custard is set and top lightly browned. Let cool in the pan on a wire rack for 15 minutes. Cut into squares. Sprinkle with powdered sugar and serve with berries or other fruit.

CINNAMON COFFEE CAKE

Servings: 10-12

This coffee cake comes from the oven with a crunchy layer of frosting on top.

1 cup butter or margarine
2 cups sugar
1 tsp. vanilla
4 eggs, separated
2½ cups flour

4 tsp. baking powder
½ tsp. salt
2 tsp. ground cinnamon
1 cup milk

Frosting
4 tbs. butter or margarine
⅔ cup powdered sugar

½ tsp. ground cinnamon

Cream butter and sugar until fluffy. Mix in vanilla and egg yolks. Combine flour, baking powder, salt and cinnamon and add to creamed mixture alternately with milk. Stir only enough to blend well. Beat egg whites until they hold soft peaks and fold them into batter. Spoon into a buttered 9 x 13 pan and bake at 350° for 45 minutes.

Cream together 4 tbs. butter, powered sugar and ½ tsp. cinnamon. Spread on top of coffee cake and return to oven for 5 minutes. Cool briefly and serve warm.

SOUR CREAM-BRAN COFFEE CAKE

Servings: 10-12

This recipe is an old timer, but the addition of bran gives it a healthy and flavorful update. Yogurt may be substituted for the sour cream.

½ cup butter or margarine, softened
1 cup sugar
2 eggs
2 cups flour
1 tsp. ground cinnamon

1 tsp baking soda
½ tsp. salt
1 cup sour cream
2 cups raisin bran cereal

Topping
1 cup flour
1 tsp cinnamon

⅔ cup brown sugar, packed
½ cup butter

Cream ½ cup butter with sugar until fluffy. Blend in eggs. In another bowl, combine 2 cups flour, 1 tsp. cinnamon, baking soda and salt; add to creamed mixture alternately with sour cream. Stir in cereal and spoon batter into a buttered 9 x 13 pan.

Combine 1 cup flour, 1 tsp. cinnamon and brown sugar. Cut in ½ cup butter until mixture forms a coarse crumb. Sprinkle over batter and bake at 350° for 35 to 40 minutes or until a tester comes out clean.

Frosting

1 cup powdered sugar   4 tbs. milk

Mix powdered sugar and milk and drizzle over hot cake. Cool briefly and serve warm.

NORWEGIAN COFFEE CAKE

Servings: 10-12

I've enjoyed this simple morning cake for so long that its provenance is no longer clear. I do seem to remember, however, that it was at one time served on a Norwegian freighter, hence the name.

1 cup sugar
6 tbs. butter or margarine
2 eggs
⅔ cup milk

2 cups flour
3 tbs. baking powder
½ tsp. salt

Filling

1 cup brown sugar, packed
4 tbs. flour
2 tsp. ground cinnamon

4 tbs. butter or margarine, melted
1 cup chopped pecans

Cream 1 cup sugar and butter until fluffy. Add eggs and mix well. Stir in milk. Combine flour, baking powder and salt and add to creamed mixture.

In another bowl combine brown sugar, 4 tbs. flour, cinnamon, melted butter, and pecans. Spread half the batter in a buttered 9 x 13 pan. Sprinkle with half the filling. Repeat. Bake at 375° for 30 to 35 minutes or until a tester comes out clean. Cool briefly and serve warm.

APPLES WITH SAUSAGE STUFFING

Servings: 10

Stuffing apples with sausage turns them into a delightful main course. These are sure favorites for breakfast or brunch and are also perfect as part of a buffet.

10 Golden Delicious, Granny Smith or other baking apples
1 lb. sweet Italian sausage or country pork sausage
2 tbs. minced parsley
2 cups dry white wine or apple cider

Cut a slice from the bottom of each apple. Core them and, with a small melon baller, scoop out insides, leaving a ¾ inch shell. Chop pulp and combine with sausage and parsley. Fill apples with mixture and place them in a 9 x 13 pan. Pour wine over apples and bake at 375° for 40 to 50 minutes or until apples are tender. Baste several times with wine during baking. Serve hot or warm with wine as sauce.

TACO QUICHE

Either purchase or make the salsa to accompany this dish. In addition, sour cream, sliced tomatoes, sliced avocados, lettuce and olives are all appropriate accompaniments.

8 corn tortillas
2 tbs. vegetable oil
2 lbs. lean ground beef
1 onion, chopped
2 cloves garlic, pressed
1 tsp. chili powder, or to taste
¼ tsp. ground cumin

¼ tsp. dried thyme
salt
½ tsp. dried oregano
1 lb. grated Jack cheese
6 eggs, beaten
2 cups milk

Line a greased 9 x 13 pan with tortillas, tearing to fit. Heat oil in a skillet and brown beef. Add onions, garlic, chili powder, cumin, thyme, oregano and salt; cook 5 minutes. Spoon mixture into tortilla-lined pan. Top with cheese. Beat eggs and milk together and pour over contents of pan. Bake at 350° for 1 hour or until custard is set. Serve warm with garnishes.

SALADS

PASTA SALAD WITH RICOTTA-WALNUT SAUCE

This salad benefits by an overnight rest in the refrigerator. Let it stand at room temperature for half an hour before serving.

¾ cup full-flavored olive oil
1½ cups coarsely chopped, toasted
  walnuts
1½ cups ricotta cheese
2 (10 oz. each) pkgs. frozen chopped
  spinach, thawed and squeezed
  very dry
¼ cup chopped parsley

2 cloves garlic, pressed
2 tsp. chopped fresh basil or ½ tsp.
  dried
3 tsp. fresh oregano or 1½ tsp. dried
1 lb. small pasta shells, cooked and
  drained
lettuce

Combine all ingredients except pasta in a large bowl. Add pasta and mix well. Refrigerate. Half an hour before serving, line a 9 x 13 pan with lettuce leaves. Spoon pasta mixture on top and let stand until ready to serve.

TACO SALAD

This is a wonderful salad for a crowd. It can easily be doubled (you'll need two dishes then) and the variations are many. If you have a decorative earthenware or other attractive 9 x 13 dish, this is a good time to use it.

1 head iceberg lettuce, shredded, or other lettuce torn into small pieces
4 cups cooked beans, red kidney, black or pinto
2 cups cooked corn kernels, fresh or frozen
2 avocados, peeled, pitted and sliced

2 lbs. lean ground beef, cooked and well drained, or 4 whole chicken breasts, poached, boned and cut into strips or ½ turkey breast, poached, boned and cut into strips
4 ripe tomatoes, peeled, seeded and quartered
3 cups grated sharp cheddar cheese

Dressing
2 cups plain yogurt
1½ cups chili sauce or salsa

½ cup beer

Line a 9 x 13 pan or serving dish with lettuce. Top with beans, then corn, then avocado, beef or poultry, tomatoes and cheese. Combine dressing ingredients well and drizzle over salad just before serving. Serve with warm tortillas or corn chips.

PEACH SALAD WITH CUCUMBERS AND TOMATOES

Terrific flavor combination. Prepare peaches at serving time, or they will darken.

Dressing

1 cup tarragon red wine vinegar
3/4 cup water
6 tbs. sugar
1 tsp. salt

6 tbs. finely chopped fresh mint
3 tbs. finely chopped preserved or
  crystalized ginger

Salad

9 fresh peaches, peeled and sliced
2 cups peeled, seeded and thinly
  sliced cucumbers
2 baskets cherry tomatoes

1 bunch green onions, thinly sliced,
  including some green
lettuce leaves
watercress for garnish

In a small saucepan, bring vinegar, water, sugar and salt to a boil. Remove from heat; add mint and ginger. Cool and refrigerate. Combine peaches, cucumbers, tomatoes and green onions. Remove mint and ginger from dressing; add to peach mixture. Toss well. Line a 9 x 13 dish with lettuce leaves. Add peach mixture. Garnish with watercress and serve dressing on the side.

SCANDINAVIAN PEACH SALAD

Servings: 10-12

This salad works well with canned peaches and peps up a winter meal. Of course, fresh peaches may be used in season.

2 (29 oz. each) cans peach slices
1 cup sour cream
1 cup plain yogurt
2 tsp. dill

½ tsp. thyme
peel of ½ lemon, finely grated
½ tsp. salt
1 head iceberg lettuce, shredded

Drain peach slices and set aside. Whisk sour cream, yogurt, dill, thyme, lemon peel and salt together until smooth. Fold in peaches. Place shredded lettuce in a 9 x 13 serving dish. Top with peach mixture. Chill until ready to serve.

CAPE COD JELLIED APPLE CIDER SALAD

This shimmering golden salad is delicious with meat or poultry. Serve it with a dollop of sour cream spiked with horseradish.

2 (3 oz. each) pkgs. lemon-flavored
  gelatin
4 cups hot apple cider
½ tsp. salt

3 tsp. lemon juice
4 large red apples, unpeeled, diced
1½ cups finely diced celery

Dissolve gelatin in hot cider. Add all other ingredients and mix well. Pour into a 9 x 13 serving dish and chill until firm, about 3 to 4 hours. Cut into squares to serve.

TOMATO ASPIC

This is one of the oldest recipes in my files and it never fails. Even though it seems a tad old-fashioned, its crisp, clean flavor makes it an all-year salad treat.

2 (46 oz. each) cans tomato juice
2/3 cup chopped onion
1/2 cup celery tops and leaves
1½ tsp. salt
pepper
3 small bay leaves
8 whole cloves
4 envelopes (4 tbs.) plain gelatin

1/2 cup cold water
6 tbs. lemon juice
2 cups finely chopped celery or peeled, seeded or chopped cucumber or combination
parsley, watercress or lemon wedges for garnish

In a nonaluminum pan, combine tomato juice with onion, celery tops, salt, pepper, bay leave and cloves. Simmer 5 minutes and strain. Soften gelatin in water. Add it to hot tomato juice and stir to dissolve completely. Add lemon juice.

When partially set, add chopped celery and/or cucumber and pour into a 9 x 13 serving dish. Chill until firm, 2 to 3 hours. Garnish with parsley, watercress or lemon wedges.

MOLDED PINK SALAD

Servings: 10-12

*This pretty salad is a natural partner with **Tomato Aspic,** page 25. I like to serve them side by side on a buffet table. This salad is also surprisingly good for brunch.*

4 envelopes (4 tbs.) plain gelatin
1 cup cold water
4 (8 oz. each) cans tomato sauce
4 (3 oz. each) pkgs. cream cheese,
  softened, or 1½ cups ricotta cheese
2 cups mayonnaise

2 cups finely chopped celery
1 cup finely chopped green onion,
  including some green
1 cup finely chopped green bell pepper
½ cup chopped green olives

In a nonaluminium saucepan, soften gelatin in water. Add tomato sauce and heat over low heat until gelatin is dissolved. Beat cream cheese with mayonnaise until smooth. Add celery, green onion, green pepper and olives. Stir vegetables into tomato mixture and combine thoroughly. Pour into a 9 x 13 serving dish and chill for 3 to 4 hours or until firm. Cut into squares to serve.

ROSE MARIE'S RICE SALAD

This recipe is not quite as given to me by my old friend, but it's close. It is also simple to prepare and very good. To make a more substantial salad, add 2 cups cooked shrimp.

4 cups cooked white rice or orzo
4 (4 oz. each) jars marinated artichoke hearts, drained (marinade reserved) and cut up
½ cup sliced pimiento-stuffed olives
2 (8 oz. each) cans water chestnuts, sliced

6 green onions, thinly sliced, including some green
⅔ cup mayonnaise
1 tsp. curry powder
lettuce

Combine rice, artichoke hearts, olives, water chestnuts and green onions. In another bowl mix together mayonnaise, curry powder and reserved marinade. Pour dressing over rice mixture and combine thoroughly. Chill slightly and serve in a lettuce-lined 9 x 13 serving dish.

CURRIED RICE AND SHRIMP SALAD

This is fine picnic fare, but it tastes good at home, too. I sometimes substitute cooked orzo or other small pasta for the rice.

4 cups cooked white rice
1 cup sliced pimiento-stuffed olives
2 cups finely chopped green or red
  bell pepper

½ cup finely chopped green onions,
  including some green
½ cup capers, drained
2 lbs. cooked small shrimp
lettuce

Dressing
3 cups mayonnaise
2-4 tsp. curry powder

juice of 1 lemon
salt and pepper

Combine rice, olives, pepper, onions, capers and shrimp. In another bowl mix together mayonnaise, curry powder, lemon juice, salt and pepper; add it to rice mixture. Toss to combine. Line a 9 x 13 serving dish with lettuce leaves. Pile dressed salad on top and serve at once. Garnish with parsley, cilantro or watercress, if desired.

BRAZILIAN BLACK BEAN SALAD

Black beans have a wonderful flavor and hold their shape well. Canned beans lessen the preparation time and may be used, but be sure to drain them well.

6 cups cooked black beans
6 tbs. vegetable oil
8 cloves garlic, sliced
3 large carrots, peeled and chopped
3 large red onions, chopped
6 stalks celery, chopped
3 green bell peppers, seeded and chopped

3 tbs. ground coriander
1½ tsp. ground cumin, or to taste
3 large navel oranges, sectioned
3 tbs. sherry vinegar
3 tbs. lemon juice
salt and pepper
lettuce
sour cream

Place beans in a large bowl and set aside. Sauté garlic in oil until it just begins to brown. Remove garlic; add carrots, onion, celery and green pepper. Stir in coriander and cumin; cook until vegetables are soft, stirring frequently. Add vegetables to beans. Over a bowl, peel oranges and cut each section in half. Let juice and sections fall into bowl. Add vinegar, lemon juice, salt and pepper. Mix well and toss with beans. Pile beans into a 9 x 13 serving dish and refrigerate until about an hour before serving. Serve chopped lettuce and sour cream on the side.

TUNA/BEAN SALAD

Servings: 10-12

White kidney beans, available canned, are often called cannellini beans. This bean salad is a fine luncheon or supper main dish.

4 (6 oz. each) cans water-packed
   chunk tuna, drained
4 (12 oz. each) cans white kidney
   beans, drained and rinsed
2 baskets cherry tomatoes, cut in half

8 stalks celery, thinly sliced on the
   diagonal
1 bunch green onions, thinly sliced,
   including some green

Dressing

2 onions, cut into chunks
8 tbs. Dijon mustard
8 tbs. sherry wine vinegar
2 tsp. salt

1 cup full-flavored olive oil
3/4 cup vegetable oil
salt and pepper

In a large bowl, combine tuna, beans, tomatoes, celery and green onions. Place the cut-up onions in a food processor and puree with the steel blade. Scrape down sides of bowl as needed. Add mustard, vinegar and salt; puree until smooth. With the machine running, slowly add oils. Add salt and pepper to taste. Gently toss dressing with tuna mixture. Line a 9 x 13 serving dish with salad greens. Pile tuna mixture on top.

MOROCCAN SALAD

This is a splendid winter salad. For a colorful change, use half navel oranges and half blood oranges and top the finished dish with thinly sliced green bell pepper rings. Full-flavored Mediterranean olives are especially appropriate here.

8 eating oranges, peeled and sliced
4 small red onions, very thinly sliced

¾ cup pitted black olives
romaine lettuce

Dressing
¾ cup full-flavored olive oil
4 cloves garlic, pressed
1 tsp. paprika
1 tsp. salt

2 tsp. Tabasco sauce
1 tsp. powdered cumin
4 tbs. lemon juice

Combine oranges, onion and olives. Whisk together oil, garlic, paprika, salt, Tabasco, cumin and lemon juice. Stir dressing gently into orange mixture; let stand 20 minutes. Line a 9 x 13 serving dish with romaine lettuce leaves. Place orange mixture on top. Serve well chilled.

MARY LYNN'S TABOULEH

Tabouleh salads are legion, but this one is definitely in a class by itself. If you double the recipe for a large crowd, you might serve the bulgar mixture in one 9 x 13 serving dish and the tomato mixture in another. It's best made the day before.

Bulgar Mixture

1 cup bulgar
¾ cup boiling water
⅔ cup minced onion
¼ cup chopped parsley
1 cup finely chopped and seeded
   cucumber

1 cup minced celery
1½ tbs. chopped fresh mint
6 tbs. full-flavored olive oil
2 tbs. lemon juice
salt and pepper

Combine bulgar and water in a large bowl. Let stand until luke warm. Add minced onion, parsley, cucumber, celery, mint, olive oil, lemon juice, salt and pepper. Chill several hours or overnight.

Tomato Mixture

2 lbs. ripe tomatoes, peeled and
  seeded
1 cup finely sliced green onion,
  including some green
1 cup diced and seeded cucumber
½ cup pitted ripe olives
¾ cup diced and seeded green bell
  pepper

1 tsp. fresh chopped basil or ½ tsp. dried
1 tsp. fresh chopped oregano or ½
  tsp. dried
¼ cup wine vinegar
½ cup full-flavored olive oil
salt and pepper
spinach or lettuce leaves
1 lb. feta cheese, crumbled

Dice tomatoes coarsely and combine with green onion, cucumber, olives, bell pepper, basil, oregano, vinegar and olive oil. Toss lightly, season with salt and pepper and chill several hours. Spoon some dressing from tomatoes over crumbled cheese and refrigerate.

When ready to serve, line a 9 x 13 serving dish with lettuce or spinach leaves. Mound bulgar in one side of dish and tomatoes in other. Garnish both with crumbled cheese.

DEVILED LENTIL SALAD

Servings: 10-12

Lentils, an often neglected food in the United States, deserve greater exposure. They are inexpensive, easy to cook, and combine well with a wide range of spices and other foods. This simple salad is good whatever the season.

2 cups uncooked lentils, washed and
  picked over
8 cups water
6 cups fresh mushrooms, thickly
  sliced
1 cup chopped green onion, including
  some green
½ cup chopped parsley
2 green or red bell peppers, cut into
  thin strips
2 tomatoes, peeled, seeded and
  chopped

4 cloves garlic, pressed
8 tbs. full-flavored olive oil
4 tbs. wine vinegar
2 tbs. Dijon mustard
4 tsp. chopped cilantro, or more to
  taste
2 tsp. chopped fresh oregano or 1
  tsp. dried
½ tsp. Worcestershire sauce
dash of Tabasco sauce
salt and pepper
lettuce or spinach leaves

Simmer lentils in water to cover for 20 minutes. Drain well and combine with mushrooms, onion, parsley, bell pepper, tomatoes and garlic. In a small bowl, whisk together oil, vinegar, mustard, cilantro, oregano, Worcestershire and Tabasco. Add salt and pepper to taste and pour dressing over lentils. Chill at least 3 hours or overnight, stirring occasionally.

Line a 9 x 13 serving dish with lettuce or spinach leaves. Pile lentils on top. Garnish with additional cilantro, if desired. For best flavor, serve at room temperature.

NORTH AFRICAN VEGETABLE SALAD

Servings: 8-10

The ingredients are not unusual, but the combination is slightly exotic — and awfully good. An easy salad to prepare early in the day, it's the perfect partner for grilled chicken, fish or meat.

1 lb. small whole mushrooms, stems trimmed
3 cups cooked garbanzo beans, well drained (canned are fine)
2 cups pitted ripe olives, drained

1½ cups coarsely chopped green onions, including some green
4 red or green bell peppers, seeded and chopped
24 cherry tomatoes

Dressing
2 cups plain yogurt
1 cup mayonnaise
4 cloves garlic, pressed
4 tbs. full-flavored olive oil

2 tbs. lemon juice
2 tsp. powdered cumin
¼ tsp. turmeric
salt and pepper

Combine mushrooms, beans, olives, green onions, peppers and cherry tomatoes; chill. Combine remaining ingredients and chill. Just before serving, lightly coat vegetables with dressing and pile into a lettuce-lined 9 x 13 serving dish. Serve remaining dressing on the side.

POULTRY ENTRÉES

BAKED CHICKEN THIGHS PROVENÇAL   Servings: 8-10

The robust flavors of Provence are easy to incorporate in any dish with the help of an herb blend called Herbes de Provence. This useful mix usually includes basil, fennel seeds, lavender, marjoram, sage, rosemary, thyme and summer savory.

3 tbs. olive oil
1 lb. mushrooms, sliced
18 chicken thighs, skinned
3 large onions, coarsely chopped
1½ tbs. flour
3 cloves garlic, minced
½ cup minced parsley

1½ tbs. Herbes de Provence
finely grated peel and juice of 1 large
  orange
3 tomatoes, peeled, seeded and
  quartered
¾ cup dry white wine
Mediterranean olives for garnish

Heat 1 tablespoon of oil and sauté mushrooms quickly for 3 to 4 minutes. Set aside. In another skillet, heat remaining oil and brown chicken on all sides. Add onions and continue to cook until onions are soft. Remove chicken pieces to a 9 x 13 pan, top with mushrooms and set aside.

Sprinkle flour over onions and mix well. Add garlic, parsley, herbs and orange peel; cook 3 to 4 minutes, stirring constantly. Add orange juice, tomatoes and wine, mix well, and bring quickly to a boil. Pour over chicken. Cover with foil and bake at 350° for 35 to 40 minutes or until chicken is done.

CHICKEN CUBAN STYLE

Servings: 12

This dish may be prepared with whatever chicken pieces you prefer. For a more elegant meal, use boned half chicken breasts.

12 chicken pieces, skin removed
6 cloves garlic
2 onions, coarsely chopped
1 green bell pepper, seeded and
  coarsely chopped
4 (5 oz.) cans tomato sauce

2 tsp. cumin seeds
3 tsp. dried oregano
2 cups raisins
1 cup pimiento-stuffed green olives
4 tbs. vegetable oil
2 tbs. white wine vinegar

Place chicken pieces in a 9 x 13 pan. Place all other ingredients in a blender or food processor and puree until smooth. Pour sauce over chicken. Cover with foil and bake at 325° for 1 hour and 15 minutes. Serve with rice.

CHICKEN POLYNESIAN

Servings: 6

I'm not sure how authentically Polynesian this recipe is, but that's what I've called it for years. Polynesian or not, it's delicious.

6 small chicken quarters
1½ cups vegetable oil
⅔ cup lemon juice
6 tbs. soy sauce

3 cloves garlic, minced
2 tsp. dried oregano
salt and pepper

Place chicken in a 9 x 13 pan. Combine remaining ingredients and pour them over chicken. Allow to marinate at least 4 to 5 hours, basting and turning chicken several times. Bake chicken at 350° in pan with marinade, skin side down, for 20 minutes. Turn chicken and bake 20 minutes longer or until chicken is done. Baste with marinade while baking. Serve hot.

GREEK CHICKEN

The sauce in this well-flavored dish is thin. To make a complete meal, add 1 cup orzo for the last 30 minutes of the cooking time.

12 half chicken breasts, or 16 thighs
  or a combination
salt and pepper
2 tbs. ground cinnamon
juice of 2 lemons

3 onions, coarsely chopped
6 tbs. vegetable oil
4 cups tomato sauce
1 cup water
1 cup orzo (optional)

Remove skin from chicken pieces. Place them in a 9 x 13 pan and add salt, pepper, cinnamon and lemon juice. Marinate chicken for 1 hour, turning several times. In a large sauté pan, brown onion in oil. Add chicken and brown each piece well. Return chicken to 9 x 13 pan. Add tomato sauce and water to sauté pan and scrape up any browned pieces. Pour over chicken. Cover with foil and bake at 300° for 1½ hours or until chicken is very tender.

If adding orzo, stir into sauce in pan; cook for last 30 minutes.

CHICKEN PARMIGIANA

Servings: 8

An old Italian favorite and a never-fail crowd pleaser.

1½ tbs. olive oil
3 tbs. finely chopped onion
3 (8 oz. each) cans tomato sauce
1½ tsp. chopped fresh basil or ½
  tsp. dried
½ tsp. salt
1 cup flour

2 eggs, well beaten
1 cup milk
8 half chicken breasts, skinned,
  boned and slightly flattened
2 tbs. olive oil
8 slices mozzarella cheese or ½ lb.
  grated

Sauté onion in oil until soft. Add tomato sauce, basil and salt; simmer 5 minutes. Set aside. Mix together flour, eggs and milk; dip chicken pieces in mixture to coat. Sauté chicken in olive oil until pieces are golden on both sides. Place chicken in a 9 x 13 pan. Pour tomato sauce over. Top with cheese and bake at 350° for 20 minutes or until chicken is done.

COUNTRY CAPTAIN

This is an old and much loved recipe which I have adapted for the 9 x 13 pan. For a more elegant dish, use boned chicken pieces. It's good hot or cold.

12 chicken legs and thighs, skinned
½ cup flour
2 tsp. curry powder
1 tsp. salt
8 tbs. butter or margarine
4 tbs. vegetable oil
⅔ cup chopped green bell pepper

4 cloves garlic, minced
2 tbs. curry powder
1 tsp. dried thyme
2 (16 oz. each) cans tomatoes
6 tbs. currants soaked in ½ cup
  brandy or water

Combine flour, 2 tsp. curry powder and salt; coat chicken pieces. Heat butter and oil together in a large skillet and brown chicken pieces well. As they brown, remove them to a 9 x 13 pan. Sauté onion, green pepper, garlic, 2 tbs. curry powder and thyme in the same skillet until vegetables are limp. Stir in tomatoes. Pour contents of skillet over chicken. Cover with foil and bake at 350° for 30 minutes or until chicken is done. Correct seasoning; add currants and brandy.

CHICKEN JEWEL

Servings: 8

This recipe really is a jewel. I'm not sure where I first discovered it, but I have used it for years and given it to many friends. A pound of fresh mushrooms may be lightly sautéed and substituted for the artichoke hearts. Or, go for broke and use both.

8 half chicken breasts, skinned and boned
2 to 4 tbs. vegetable oil
2 (4 oz. each) jars marinated artichoke hearts
8 slices Swiss cheese

Between 2 pieces of waxed paper, flatten chicken to uniform thickness. In a skillet, heat oil and brown chicken pieces lightly on each side. Arrange them in a single layer in a lightly greased 9 x 13 pan. Drain artichoke hearts (reserve liquid to add to tossed salads) and chop coarsely. Discard any tough leaves. Spoon artichokes on top of chicken. Top with cheese and bake at 350° for about 20 minutes or until chicken is done and cheese is melted.

BROCCOLI-PEACH CHICKEN

Servings: 8-12

An interesting combination of flavors give this dish top honors. It's attractive, too. Nectarines may be substituted for the peaches.

12 half chicken breasts, skinned and
  boned
salt and pepper
1 cup butter or margarine
1 cup finely chopped green onions,
  including some green
4 cloves garlic, minced

3 tsp. paprika
3 bunches broccoli, trimmed and
  freshly cooked
12 peach halves, peeled, or canned
3 cups sour cream or plain yogurt
¾ cup mayonnaise
¾ cup grated Parmesan cheese

Sprinkle chicken with salt and pepper. Melt butter in a large sauté pan; sauté green onions and garlic for 2 to 3 minutes. Stir in paprika and turn chicken pieces in mixture until each piece is well coated. Place chicken in a lightly greased 9 x 13 pan. Pour any onions remaining in sauté pan over chicken. Cover loosely with foil and bake at 375° for 25 minutes. Arrange well-drained broccoli and peaches around chicken. Mix together sour cream and mayonnaise; spoon over all. Sprinkle with Parmesan cheese. Broil 6 inches from heat for 6 to 8 minutes or until top is glazed and flecked with brown. Serve immediately.

CHICKEN WITH ARTICHOKE HEARTS

Servings: 6

Chicken and artichoke hearts are a wonderful flavor combination. This dish reheats well.

6 chicken breasts, skinned and boned
1 tsp. salt
½ tsp. pepper
½ tsp. paprika
4 tbs. butter or margarine
3 cups sliced mushrooms
4 tbs. butter or margarine

1 tsp. tarragon
2 tbs. flour
½ cup dry sherry
1¼ cups chicken stock
3 (3 oz. each) jars marinated
   artichoke hearts, drained
chopped parsley

Pat chicken dry, sprinkle with salt, pepper, and paprika, and sauté in 4 tbs. butter until browned. Remove to a 9 x 13 pan. Sauté mushrooms in 4 tbs. butter. Sprinkle on flour and tarragon. Add sherry and stock; bring to a boil. Simmer 3 to 4 minutes, stirring constantly. Arrange artichoke hearts around chicken in pan. Pour sauce over chicken and bake at 350° for 40 to 45 minutes or until chicken is done. Sprinkle with chopped parsley to serve.

DALE'S CHICKEN

My friend Dale, who gave me this recipe, calls it "Chicken in the White Dish," but any color dish does nicely for this main course that is quickly put together, thanks to prepared ingredients.

1 cup regular rice, uncooked
1 (4 lbs.) chicken, cut into pieces
1 (10¾ oz.) can cream of mushroom
  soup
1 (1 oz.) pkg. dry onion soup mix

1 (10¾ oz.) soup can of water
1 cup thinly sliced onions (optional)
1 cup thinly sliced mushrooms
  (optional)

Place rice in a 9 x 13 baking dish and top with chicken pieces. Pour mushroom soup over chicken and sprinkle onion soup mix over contents of dish. Top with sliced onions and mushrooms, if desired. Pour 1 soup can of water over all. Cover dish tightly with foil and bake at 375° for about 1 hour or until rice has absorbed all liquid and chicken is done. Add more water during baking if chicken cooks more slowly than rice. Remove foil the last 15 minutes to allow chicken to brown.

CANNELLONI A LA CALIFORNIA

Servings: 8

This do-ahead entrée is worth the time it takes. Make it either with crepes (recipe follows) or with flour tortillas. Made with crepes, it's a more delicate dish.

5 cups cooked, boned chicken, finely chopped
1½ cups chopped onion
2 cloves garlic, minced
2 tsp. fresh oregano or 1 tsp. dried
3 tsp. fresh basil or 1 tsp. dried
1 tsp. fresh sage or ½ tsp. dried

salt and pepper
1 cup minced parsley
2 cups grated Parmesan cheese
white sauce
red sauce
2 cups grated Jack cheese

White Sauce

6 tbs. butter or margarine
6 tbs. flour
3½ cups half and half

salt and pepper
½ tsp. grated nutmeg

Red Sauce

½ cup minced onion
2 tbs. olive oil

1 tsp. fresh basil or ½ tsp. dried
2 (8 oz. each) cans tomato sauce

Combine chicken with onion, garlic, oregano, basil, sage, salt, pepper and parsley. Mix in 1 cup white sauce and 1 cup Parmesan cheese. Lay 16 crepes or tortillas flat and spoon chicken mixture on each. Roll up. Spread a thin layer of white sauce in the bottom of a 9 x 13 pan. Place filled crepes, seam side down, in sauce. Spoon red sauce in wide lengthwise strips across crepes. Pour remaining white sauce in narrow bands over red sauce. Sprinkle with remaining Parmesan and top all with Jack cheese. Bake at 350° for 30 minutes. Sprinkle with additional chopped parsley at serving time, if desired. If made ahead, bring to room temperature before heating.

Crepes That Never Fail

This recipe is different from most in that it uses granular flour and the batter can be used immediately. Makes about 20 six-inch crepes.

1½ cups *granular* flour
1 cup cold water
1 cup cold milk

4 large eggs
½ tsp. salt
4 tbs. melted butter or margarine

With a wire whisk, gradually blend water, milk, eggs, salt and butter into flour. When smooth, cook in a lightly buttered slope-sided skillet over medium high heat. When lightly brown on the bottom, turn to dry other side. Cool in a rack and then stack between pieces of waxed paper. Can be frozen.

CUBAN CHICKEN PIE

*Bake this savory and unusual filling under a **Flaky Pastry Crust**, page 135, or use puff pastry to create a more glamorous entrée.*

2 green bell peppers, seeded and
  chopped
4 tbs. olive oil
½ cup tomato sauce
6 green onions, minced, including
  some green
salt and pepper
2 bay leaves
2 cups water

4 cups cooked, diced chicken, skin
  and bones removed
½ cup dry white wine
½ cup raisins
1 cup pimiento-stuffed green olives
  cut in half
1 cup frozen peas
2 (2 oz. each) jars diced pimiento

In a large skillet, sauté green peppers in oil until they are limp. Add all remaining ingredients and mix well. Transfer mixture to a 9 x 13 pan. Cover top with pastry and crimp edges. Cut several slits in top to let steam escape. Bake at 400° for 20 minutes or until crust is golden. Cut into squares to serve.

SEAFOOD ENTRÉES

FISH SOUFFLÉS FLORENTINE

Servings: 12

An unusual way to serve fish fillets. The soufflés will not fall — even the next day.

4 green onions, chopped, including
  some green
2 tsp. butter or margarine
3 bunches spinach, chopped
salt, pepper and grated nutmeg
½ cup grated Parmesan cheese

2½ lbs. fillets of firm-fleshed white
  fish (sole, snapper, halibut)
8 eggs, separated
2 tsp. grated lemon peel
1 tsp. dry mustard
⅔ cup sour cream
4 egg whites

In a large sauté pan, cook onions in butter until they are soft. Add spinach and cook until it is just wilted. Season with salt, pepper and nutmeg; mix in cheese. Spoon spinach mixture into a greased 9 x 13 pan. Season fish with salt and pepper; place fillets on top of spinach. Beat egg yolks with lemon peel and mustard until thick. Mix in sour cream. Beat 12 egg whites until they hold soft peaks and fold them into egg yolk mixture. Spread over fish and bake at 375° for 20 minutes or until puffed and golden. Serve hot.

BAKED SALMON WITH
MUSTARD LEMON SAUCE

Servings: 8

Fresh salmon steaks are always a treat — especially so with this savory sauce.

8 salmon steaks
1 cup minced green onions, including
  some green
1 cup minced celery

1 cup minced parsley
2 tbs. dry mustard
2 cups dry vermouth
4 tbs. butter or margarine

Rinse salmon steaks and pat dry. In a lightly greased 9 x 13 pan, place onions, celery and parsley. Arrange salmon steaks on top. Combine dry mustard and vermouth and pour over contents of pan. Cover with foil and bake at 350° for about 35 minutes or until fish flakes easily. Remove from oven, and with a long-handled spoon, remove as much of liquid as possible to a saucepan. Cook it quickly to reduce to sauce consistency. Add butter; when melted, pour sauce over fish. Serve immediately, making sure each serving includes some of the vegetables.

GOURMET FINNAN HADDIE

Servings: 12

Finnan haddie is seldom eaten outside New England, and that's too bad. This is a wonderful dish for brunch, lunch or supper. Finnan haddie with bone in may need to be special-ordered. It has more flavor than the boned fillets, but use either.

2 (3 lb. each) finnan haddie, bone in,
　or 6 lbs. fillets
4 cups milk, about
8 tbs. butter or margarine
1/2 onion, minced
1 green bell pepper, seeded and minced
1 red bell pepper, seeded and minced

1/2 tsp. salt
3/4 cup flour
1 tsp. paprika
dash cayenne
2 cups heavy cream
2 cups half and half
1 cup dry bread crumbs, buttered

Place fish in a 9 x 13 pan (you may need 2 pans for this part of the recipe) and cover with milk. Allow to sit for 1 hour. Place pans in a 350° oven and bake until fish flakes easily, about 20 minutes. Set aside. Melt butter in a skillet and sauté onion and peppers for 5 minutes. Add salt, flour, paprika and cayenne; stir until smooth. Add 4 cups of milk drained from fish, heavy cream and half and half. Cook and whisk until sauce begins to boil and thickens slightly. Remove from heat. Flake fish. Wash, dry and lightly grease one 9 x 13 pan.

Combine fish and sauce; pour it into prepared pan. Cover top with crumbs and heat in a 400° oven for 10 to 15 minutes or until crumbs have browned slightly. Serve over toast, if desired.

SCALLOPS WITH SAVORY CRUMBS

Servings: 8

An unusual lemon-thyme "pesto" tops scallops in this quick and easy dish.

3 lbs. scallops
juice of 2 lemons
8 tbs. butter or margarine, room
  temperature

½ cup lemon-thyme pesto
1 cup dry bread crumbs, about
salt
lemon wedges

Preheat oven to 450°. Place scallops in an even layer in a lightly greased 9 x 13 pan. Sprinkle lemon juice over scallops. Combine butter with pesto and add enough crumbs to make a crumbly texture. Add salt, if needed. Sprinkle pesto mixture over scallops and bake until bubbly, about 10 minutes. Serve with lemon wedges.

Lemon-Thyme Pesto

6 (2-inch each) strips lemon peel
1½ cups fresh parsley
4 tbs. dried thyme
4 cloves garlic

4 tbs. lemon juice
½ cup pine nuts
¾ cup olive oil
salt and pepper

In a blender or food processor, puree lemon peel, parsley, thyme, garlic, lemon juice and pine nuts. With the motor running, add olive oil in a thin stream. Season with salt and pepper. Let stand 5 minutes before using. This is also delicious on broiled fish.

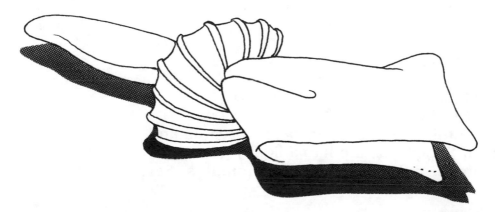

ANN'S SCALLOPS

Servings: 8

Scallops prepared this way are as rich as they are delicious. Serve them with a big green salad for a quick and easy, but elegant, meal.

2 lbs. scallops
2 cups crushed soda cracker crumbs
12 tbs. butter or margarine, melted
salt and pepper
½ tsp. paprika
1 large clove garlic, pressed
6 tbs. heavy cream
¾ cup crushed soda cracker crumbs

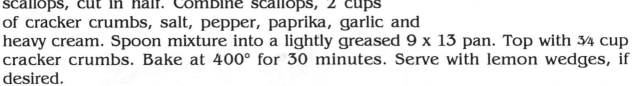

Rinse scallops and pat dry. If using sea scallops, cut in half. Combine scallops, 2 cups of cracker crumbs, salt, pepper, paprika, garlic and heavy cream. Spoon mixture into a lightly greased 9 x 13 pan. Top with ¾ cup cracker crumbs. Bake at 400° for 30 minutes. Serve with lemon wedges, if desired.

NOODLE-CRAB CASSEROLE

Servings: 6-8

Simple and delicious, this casserole travels and reheats well.

1 (6 oz.) pkg. wide noodles
2 (10¾ oz. each) cans cream of
  mushroom soup
1 lb. crab meat, picked over
1 green bell pepper, seeded and finely
  chopped

2 tsp. curry powder
¼ cup dry sherry
1 cup dry bread crumbs
1 cup grated sharp cheddar cheese

Cook noodles until done and drain well. Place them in a lightly greased 9 x 13 pan. Warm soup in a saucepan. Stir in crab, green pepper and curry powder. Mix gently but well. Stir in sherry and spoon mixture over noodles. Top with bread crumbs and then with cheese. Bake at 350° for 30 minutes.

CREOLE BAKE

This flavorful dish combines ham and shrimp in true Creole style. One jalapeño chili is about right for most people, but use more or less according to your taste.

3 tbs. vegetable oil
2 large onions, chopped
2 green bell peppers, seeded and
  chopped
1 jalapeño chili, seeded and minced
3 large cloves garlic, minced
1 (28 oz.) can crushed tomatoes,
  with liquid

1½ cups cooked ham, cubed
½ cup chicken stock or water
1 bay leaf
1 tsp. dried thyme
cayenne pepper
salt and pepper
1 lb. raw shrimp, peeled and deveined
cooked rice

Heat oil in a large skillet and sauté onion, green pepper and jalapeño until vegetables are wilted. Add garlic and cook 2 minutes. Add tomatoes, ham, stock, bay leaf, thyme, cayenne, salt and pepper.

Transfer to a 9 x 13 pan and cover with foil. Bake at 350° for 45 minutes. Stir in shrimp and bake an additional 5 minutes. Serve immediately over freshly cooked rice.

SEAFOOD LASAGNA

Many people, I've found, refer to their 9 x 13 pan as "the lasagna pan." Here's an unusual recipe for that old favorite.

½ lb. lasagna noodles, cooked
2 cups cottage cheese
1 (8 oz.) pkg. cream cheese, softened
1 cup chopped green onions, including
  some green
1 egg, beaten
2 tsp. minced fresh basil or 1 tsp. dried

salt and pepper
2 (10¾ oz. each) cans cream of
  shrimp soup
1½ lb. crab meat, picked over
¾ lb. small cooked shrimp
1 cup grated sharp cheddar cheese
1 cup grated mozzarella cheese

Combine cottage cheese, cream cheese, onion, egg, basil, salt, pepper, soup, crab and shrimp. Line a greased 9 x 13 pan with half the noodles. Top with half the seafood mixture. Repeat. Bake at 350° for 15 minutes. Top with grated cheeses and bake for 45 minutes longer. Let stand 15 minutes before cutting into squares to serve.

MEAT ENTRÉES

STIFADO

This robust Greek stew is one of my favorites. Because the meat is not browned first, it goes together quickly. Use a heavy duty pan for this recipe.

6 lbs. lean beef stew meat, cut into
  1½-inch cubes
salt and pepper
1 cup butter or margarine
5 lbs. pearl onions, peeled
2 (6 oz. each) cans tomato paste
1 cup red wine
4 tbs. red wine vinegar

2 tbs. brown sugar
2 cloves garlic, minced
2 bay leaves
2 (2-inch each) cinnamon sticks,
  broken in half
1 tsp. whole cloves
½ tsp. ground cumin
4 tbs. currants

Season meat with salt and pepper. Place butter in a heavy duty 9 x 13 pan and melt butter in a 275° oven. Add meat and onions and stir to coat with butter. In a bowl, combine tomato paste, wine, vinegar, sugar, garlic, bay leaves, cinnamon sticks, cloves, cumin and currants. Pour this mixture over meat and onions. Cover tightly with foil. Return pan to a 275° oven and bake for about 3 hours or until meat is very tender. Serve with rice or orzo.

MOUSSAKA

In this country, moussaka is probably one of the best known and best loved of the dishes from the Greek cuisine. This is my favorite version.

Meat Sauce

2 lbs. lean ground beef
2 tbs. olive oil
2 onions, finely chopped
3 tbs. tomato paste
1/2 cup dry red wine

2 large eggplants, unpeeled
6 tbs. olive oil
8 tbs. butter or margarine
1/2 cup flour
4 cups milk
1 tsp. salt

3 tbs. minced parsley
salt and pepper
1/4 tsp. ground cinnamon
1/4 tsp. allspice
2 cloves garlic, minced

1/4 tsp. grated nutmeg
pepper
5 eggs, well beaten
1/4 cup dry bread crumbs
1 cup grated Parmesan cheese

Sauté beef in oil in a large skillet. When browned, add onions and continue cooking until they are golden. Add tomato paste, wine, parsley, salt, pepper, cinnamon, allspice and garlic. Cover and simmer for 45 minutes or until sauce is very thick.

Cut eggplants across in ¾-inch slices. Place on a well-oiled baking sheet and brush both sides of each slice with oil. Bake at 400° for 30 minutes, turning once.

Melt butter in a saucepan and blend in flour. Cook 2 minutes and then gradually whisk in milk. Stir over low heat until thickened. Add salt, nutmeg and pepper; blend sauce into beaten eggs.

Arrange half the eggplant slices in a greased 9 x 13 pan. Combine meat sauce with crumbs and spread half over eggplant. Sprinkle with half the cheese. Cover with another layer of eggplant and remaining meat sauce. Spoon custard sauce over the top and sprinkle with remaining cheese. Bake at 350° for 50 to 60 minutes or until custard is set and nicely browned. Let stand 15 minutes before cutting into squares.

MEAT STEW IN A 9 X 13 PAN

Servings: 8-10

This is a method rather than a recipe. Various kinds of meat may be used, and with them various liquids and seasonings. A very easy way to make a fine meal.

2 lbs. boneless meat, well trimmed, cut in 1½-inch pieces
1 cup liquid
3 tsp. dried herbs
salt and pepper

10 cloves garlic, peeled and left whole
1 large onion, chopped
1 bay leaf
cooked rice or pasta

In a 9 x 13 pan, combine meat, liquid, herbs, salt, pepper, garlic, onion and bay leaf. Cover and let marinate in the refrigerator at least 3 hours or overnight. Stir occasionally. Bring to room temperature. Cover with foil and bake at 325° for 3 to 3½ hours or until meat is very tender. Serve with rice or pasta.

Good Combinations

- beef, half stock, half soy sauce, Herbes de Provence; might also add ripe olives and/or tomatoes

- pork, orange juice, oregano, cumin; might also add chopped green bell pepper or jalapeño and serve with black beans

- lamb, stock, marjoram, oregano, rosemary; tomatoes or potatoes

SWEET AND SOUR MEATBALLS

Servings: 8-10

Unusual and delicious, these meatballs make equally good entrée or appetizer fare, depending on the size you make them.

3 slices bread (white or whole
  wheat), crusts removed
2 lbs. lean ground beef
1 onion, minced
1 tsp. salt
pepper
½ tsp. paprika
1 egg

½ cup ice water
2 cups canned crushed tomatoes
10 gingersnaps, crumbled
½ cup brown sugar, packed
½ cup white sugar
juice of 2 lemons
lemon slices

Soak bread in cold water and squeeze dry. Mix beef, onion, salt, pepper, paprika, eggs, bread and ice water thoroughly and form into small balls. Pour tomatoes into a 9 x 13 pan. Add gingersnaps, sugars and lemon juice. Add meatballs and stir to coat with sauce.

Cover pan with foil and bake at 325° for 2 hours. Check and stir occasionally. When done, meatballs should be glazed and sauce thickened. Serve with very thin slices of lemon.

MIN'S STUFFED CABBAGE

Serves a crowd

This is a wonderful sweet-sour dish and a large recipe that will fill two 9 x 13 pans. It takes time to prepare, but it's definitely worth the effort once or twice a year. These are best reheated the next day and they freeze well. Serve with corn bread.

1 large leafy green cabbage
1 lb. lean ground beef
1 cup cooked rice
1 tsp. minced onion
2 cloves garlic, minced
salt, pepper and paprika
1 apple, peeled and cored

2 onions
1 cup brown sugar, lightly packed
1 (28 oz.) can tomatoes
1 (6 oz.) can tomato paste
½ cup honey
juice of 3 lemons
salt, pepper

Boil the whole cabbage in water to cover for 10 minutes. Carefully remove as many leaves as possible. Combine beef, rice, onion, garlic, salt, pepper and paprika. Place a large spoonful on each cabbage leaf. Fold ends over and roll up into a sausage-like roll. Use a wooden toothpick to secure. Set aside.

Cut up heart of cabbage, apple and two onions. Mix together and spread half the mixture in each of two 9 x 13 pans. Arrange cabbage rolls on top. Combine brown sugar, tomatoes, tomato paste, honey and lemon juice; pour over all. Cover pans with foil and bake at 300° until more juices have formed, about 30 minutes. Raise temperature to 325° and remove foil. Continue to bake for 2½ hours, basting with pan juices every 20 minutes.

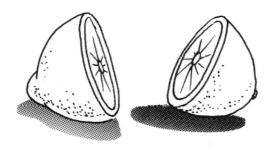

PICADILLO PIE

Picadillo is a Central and South American dish of which there are many versions. This one features a wide range of ingredients and makes an almost complete meal.

2 lbs. lean ground beef
2 cups chopped onion
2 tbs. vegetable oil
2 (16 oz. each) cans whole tomatoes,
  drained and chopped
2 (4 oz. each) cans diced green chilies
1 cup raisins
2 tbs. wine vinegar
salt

1 tsp. ground cinnamon
dash ground cloves
1 cup slivered almonds
2 (2¼ oz. each) cans sliced ripe olives,
  drained
1 cup grated sharp cheddar cheese
Flaky Pastry to cover top, page 135
cilantro

Sauté beef and onion in oil until meat is browned. Add tomatoes, chilies, raisins, vinegar, salt, cinnamon, cloves, almonds and olives; mix well. Spoon into a 9 x 13 pan, sprinkle with cheese and top with pastry. Crimp edges and cut 2 or 3 slits in top for steam to escape. Brush with beaten egg. Bake at 400° for 30 minutes, basting occasionally with egg, or until crust is richly browned. Cut into squares to serve, garnished with cilantro.

GROUND LAMB WELLINGTON

Servings: 10-12

I invented this dish as an alternative when Beef Wellington was all the rage. It's much more reliable than its more pricy cousin.

8 tbs. butter or margarine
12 large mushrooms, minced
1 large onion, minced
2 cups pitted ripe olives, minced
  (preferably a Mediterranean variety)
1 cup minced ham
2 lbs. lean ground lamb
1 tsp. marjoram

1 tsp. ground cumin
1 tsp. ground coriander
4 tbs. minced parsley
1 tsp. salt
pepper
2 sheets puff pastry
1 egg, beaten

Heat butter and sauté mushrooms, onion, olives and ham until onion is soft. Set aside.

Combine lamb, marjoram, cumin, coriander, parsley, salt and pepper; mix well. Form into 2 loaves. Place each loaf on a sheet of puff pastry and spread each evenly with ham mixture. Roll pastry sheets and crimp to seal ends. Place seam side down in a well-greased 9 x 13 pan and brush loaves with beaten egg. Bake at 375° for 20 to 25 minutes or until pastry is puffed and golden. Let stand 5 minutes before slicing.

TOURTIERE

This French-Canadian dish is traditionally served after midnight mass on Christmas Eve, but it's too good to be reserved for but once a year.

4 tbs. vegetable oil
4 onions, minced
2 cloves garlic, minced
4 tomatoes, peeled, seeded and
  chopped (if canned, drain well)
3 lbs. lean ground pork
salt and pepper
½ tsp. ground cloves

½ tsp. ground cinnamon
1 tsp. dried savory
⅔ cup minced parsley
½ cup water
½ to 1 cup dry bread crumbs
Flaky Pastry to cover top, page 135
1 egg, lightly beaten

Heat oil and add onions, garlic and about 2 cups water. Bring to a boil and cook until water has evaporated and onions are soft. Stir in tomatoes. Mix in meat and cook over medium heat, stirring occasionally, until all traces of pink have gone from meat. Stir in salt, pepper, cloves, cinnamon, savory, parsley and ½ cup water. Continue cooking over medium heat for 15 to 20 minutes, or until mixture is almost dry.

Remove from heat and stir in ½ cup bread crumbs. Allow to stand for 10 minutes and if all moisture has not been absorbed, add a few more crumbs. Spoon mixture into a lightly greased 9 x 13 pan. Top with pastry and crimp edges. Make 2 or 3 slits for steam to escape. Brush with beaten egg and bake at 450° for 10 minutes. Reduce heat to 350° and continue baking for 25 minutes, brushing occasionally with egg, or until crust is richly browned. Cut into squares to serve.

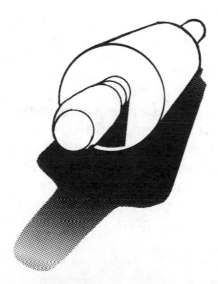

BEEF OR LAMB BOREKS

Servings: 10-12

*Boreks are Turkish savory pies which are filled with meat, vegetables or cheese. In this adaptation, filling is spread in a 9 x 13 pan and topped with a puff pastry crust which makes a beautiful presentation. Frozen puff pastry is available in most supermarkets. If you prefer, use **Flaky Pastry**, page 135.*

2 lbs. lean ground beef or lamb
8 tbs. butter or margarine
2 large onions, minced
2 green bell peppers, seeded and
  minced
2 tomatoes, peeled, seeded and
  chopped

2 cups minced parsley
4 tbs. pine nuts
4 tbs. currants
salt and pepper
6 eggs, lightly beaten

Sauté meat in butter with onions, peppers and tomatoes, stirring occasionally for 30 minutes. Remove from heat and add parsley, pine nuts, currants, salt, pepper and eggs. Mix well. Let cool; then spread in a 9 x 13 pan. Top with a single sheet of puff pastry (thawed according to package instructions and rolled to 10 x 14 inches). Crimp around edges, cut 2 or 3 slits in the top for steam to escape, and brush with 1 egg beaten with 1 tsp. water. Bake at 350° for 20 minutes or until top is puffed and golden. Cut into squares to serve.

CHEESE BOREK

Here is a cheese version.

½ lb. cream cheese
½ lb. feta cheese
2 cups cottage cheese
4 egg yolks
½ cup minced parsley

½ cup finely chopped green onions,
  including some green
salt and pepper
½ lb. Swiss cheese, grated

In a food processor, puree cream cheese, feta cheese, cottage cheese and egg yolks until smooth. Stir in parsley, green onions, salt, pepper and Swiss cheese. Spoon into a 9 x 13 pan and top with a single sheet of puff pastry (thawed according to package instructions and rolled to 10 x 14 inches). Crimp around edges, cut 2 or 3 slits in top for steam to escape, and brush with 1 egg beaten with 1 tsp. water. Bake at 350° for 20 minutes or until top is puffed and golden. Let stand 15 minutes before cutting into squares to serve.

CHILI BEANS AND MAC CASSEROLE

Servings: 8-10

This is "nothing fancy," but very good — an old-timer from my files.

2 tbs. vegetable oil
2 onions, chopped
1½ lbs. lean ground beef (or turkey)
1 tbs. chili powder, or to taste
1½ cups grated sharp cheddar cheese
2 (27 oz. each) cans kidney beans,
  undrained

1 (28 oz.) can crushed tomatoes
1½ cups pitted ripe olives
¾ cup *uncooked* elbow macaroni
½ cup grated sharp cheddar cheese

Sauté onion in oil until soft. Add beef and cook until it is no longer pink. Drain off any excess fat and add chili powder, 1½ cups cheese, beans, tomatoes, olives and uncooked macaroni. Spoon mixture into a 9 x 13 pan. It will be very moist; the macaroni will absorb the moisture. Top with ½ cup grated cheese and bake at 350° for 1 hour.

COUNTRY PATÉ

These well flavored loaves are good either hot or cold — or, best of all, at room temperature. They are ideal for picnics served with crusty bread and little pickles.

4 onions, chopped
4 tbs. butter or margarine
6 lbs. ground meat; a combination of
  veal, pork and beef is best with
  proportions in that order
8 cloves garlic, minced
4 tbs. dry sherry
salt and pepper
2 tsp. dried thyme

2 tsp. allspice
1 tsp. ground ginger
1 tsp. ground cloves
2/3 cup nonfat dry milk
6 to 8 eggs
10 slices ham, cut in 1-inch strips
1 1/3 cups sunflower seeds
10 bay leaves

Sauté onions in butter until soft; let cool. Combine meats, onions, garlic, sherry, salt, pepper, thyme, allspice, ginger, cloves and dry milk; mix well. Add as many eggs as needed to make a moist loaf mixture, but not too moist to keep its shape. With half of mixture, form 2 loaves in a 9 x 13 pan. Cover with strips of ham and sprinkle with sunflower seeds. Top with remaining meat to form 2 loaves. Press bay leaves on top to decorate. Bake at 350° for 1 1/2 hours or until set. Let stand 20 minutes before cutting.

TAGLIARINI

Servings: 10-12

This recipe goes back to my childhood. I know now that tagliarini is a shape of pasta, but we made this dish with wide egg noodles, called it tagliarini and always welcomed its appearance at dinner.

3 onions, chopped
2 cloves garlic, minced
3 tbs. olive oil
1 green bell pepper, seeded and
  chopped
1 (28 oz.) can tomatoes, undrained
1½ lbs. lean ground beef
1 (12 oz.) pkg. wide egg noodles,
  cooked and drained

1 (6 oz.) can pitted ripe olives
1 (17 oz.) can whole kernel corn or
  1½ cups frozen
salt and pepper
1 lb. sharp cheddar cheese, sliced
  thin or grated

Sauté onions and garlic in 1 tbs. oil until limp. Add green pepper and tomatoes; cook slowly for 30 minutes. Sauté beef in remaining 2 tbs. oil until it is no longer pink. Combine onions and garlic with meat. Add noodles, olives, corn, salt and pepper. Spoon half the mixture into a 9 x 13 pan. Cover with half the cheese. Repeat. Bake at 300° for 1 hour.

PORK AND RED CABBAGE WITH APPLES Servings: 8-10

This old German recipe is an ideal way to add new life to leftover pork roast. Or, you may use cooked pork chops. In either case, trim the meat well of fat.

1 lb. cooked boneless pork, cut in
  bite-sized pieces
2 lbs. red cabbage
3 tart apples, peeled, cored and cut up
2 tsp. salt

pepper
1½ tsp. caraway seeds
¼ cup sugar
3 tbs. cider vinegar, or to taste

Shred cabbage and discard thick core. Combine it with apples, salt, pepper and caraway seeds. Add pork, sugar and vinegar. Spoon into a 9 x 13 pan and cover with foil. Bake at 300° for about 30 minutes or until cabbage is crisp-tender.

SAVORY STUFFED APPLES

These pork-stuffed apples make a wonderful cold weather supper.

⅔ cup blanched slivered almonds
2 tbs. butter or margarine
1 cup chopped onion
⅔ cup chopped celery
1 lb. ground pork
1⅓ cups cranberries
4 cups fresh bread crumbs

4 tbs. currants
4 tbs. brandy or apple juice
1 tsp. crumbled sage
½ tsp. dried thyme
12 medium baking apples (Fuji, Golden Delicious)
1 cup chicken stock

Spread almonds in a single layer on a baking sheet and bake at 375° for about 5 minutes or until golden. Stir occasionally and do not allow to burn. Cool.

Melt butter and sauté onion and celery until soft. Stir in pork and cook until well browned. Stir in cranberries and cook 1 minute. Remove from heat and drain off any excess fat. Stir in bread crumbs, currants, brandy, parsley, sage, thyme and almonds. Set aside.

Cut ½ inch from top of each apple. Core and scoop insides, leaving a ¾-inch shell. (A small melon baller works well for this.) Chop 2 cups of apple pulp and add to pork mixture. Mound stuffing into apples. Place them in a 9 x 13 pan and spoon any extra stuffing around apples. Sprinkle chicken stock over all. Cover with foil and bake at 375° for 30 minutes. Remove foil and bake 15 minutes longer. Serve warm.

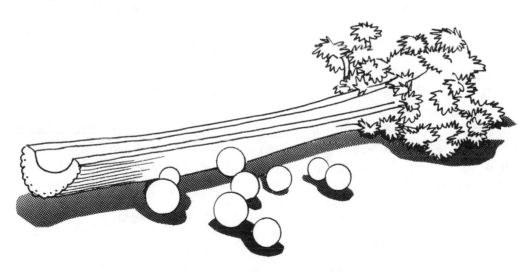

BEEF CASSEROLE WITH OLIVES

This is a hearty one-dish meal.

2 lbs. boneless chuck
1½ tbs. vegetable oil
3 tbs. red wine vinegar
3 cloves garlic, minced
salt and pepper

½ tsp. dried thyme
1 bay leaf
3 onions, thinly sliced
1½ cups pitted ripe olives
3 potatoes, peeled and thinly sliced

Trim meat and slice across the grain into 1½-inch strips about ½-inch thick. Combine ½ tbs. oil, vinegar, garlic, salt, pepper, thyme and bay leaf. Add meat, mix well, cover and marinate at least 4 hours. In a skillet, sauté onions in remaining oil until they are soft but not browned. Combine drained meat, olives, onions and potatoes; spoon into a 9 x 13 pan. Cover with foil and bake at 350° for about 2½ hours or until meat is very tender. Remove cover during the last 15 minutes.

WILD RICE CASSEROLE WITH BEEF

Servings: 10-12

This old favorite needs only a big tossed salad and a light dessert to complete the meal.

8 cups boiling water
4 cups wild rice
1½ lbs. lean ground beef
2 tbs. vegetable oil
3 (10¾ oz. each) cans chicken rice
  soup

1 lb. mushrooms, sliced
1½ cups water
¾ cup chopped onion
salt and pepper
½ lb. feta cheese, crumbled

Pour boiling water over wild rice and let stand 15 minutes. Drain. Sauté beef in oil until it is no longer pink. Drain off any excess fat. Combine rice, meat, soup, mushrooms, 1½ cups water, onion, celery, salt and pepper. Spoon into a lightly greased 9 x 13 pan. Bake at 325° for 45 minutes. Sprinkle with crumbled feta cheese and bake 15 minutes longer.

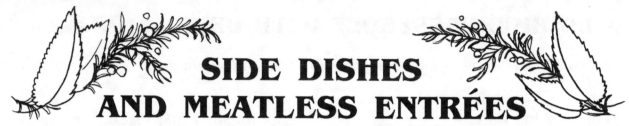

SIDE DISHES
AND MEATLESS ENTRÉES

SCALLOPED POTATOES IN WINE

Servings: 8-10

These are scalloped potatoes in the deluxe category.

8-10 red or white new potatoes,
  peeled and thinly sliced, about 6 cups
⅔ cup dry white wine
⅔ cup chicken stock
4 tbs. butter or margarine, melted

1 bunch green onions, sliced thin,
  including some green
¾ tsp. dill
2 eggs
¾ cup heavy cream

Place sliced potatoes in a greased 9 x 13 pan. Combine wine, stock, butter, onions and dill; pour over potatoes. Bake at 400° for 40 to 45 minutes. Stir once or twice so top doesn't become too brown. Beat together eggs and cream; pour over top. Continue to bake for another 20 minutes or until top is crusty and liquid is absorbed.

SAVORY POTATOES AU GRATIN

Servings: 10-12

These cheesy potatoes go well with most meat and poultry dishes and are a winning way to use leftover potatoes.

8 tbs. butter or margarine
¼ cup sliced green onions, including some green
¼ cup bottled pimiento strips, undrained
½ cup seeded and chopped green bell pepper

1 tbs. chopped parsley
1 tsp. paprika
6 cups *cooked* potato cubes
½ lb. grated sharp cheddar cheese

Sauté onions, pimiento and green pepper in butter for 2 to 3 minutes. Add parsley, paprika, potatoes and 1 cup of the cheese and stir until cheese melts. Spoon into a 9 x 13 pan. Top with remaining cheese and bake at 350° for 30 to 45 minutes or until cheese is bubbly.

SWEET POTATO CASSEROLE

Servings: 10-12

Here are sweet potatoes truly elegant. This is a fine dish with roast pork or ham.

4 large sweet potatoes
½ cup brown or white sugar
½ cup butter or margarine

2 eggs, beaten
1 tsp. vanilla
⅓ cup milk

Topping

⅓ cup melted butter or margarine
1 cup brown sugar, lightly packed

½ cup flour
1 cup chopped pecans

Peel sweet potatoes and boil them until they are done. Drain and mash. Add brown or white sugar, ½ cup butter, eggs, vanilla and milk. Combine well and spoon into a buttered 9 x 13 baking dish. Mix topping ingredients and sprinkle over potatoes. Bake at 350° for 25 minutes.

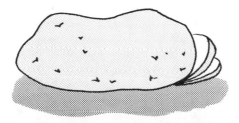

ITALIAN SPINACH AND MOZZARELLA PIE Servings: 6-8

This pie can be made with or without the pastry. The unusual flavor combination is surprising and delightful.

1/4 cup olive oil
1/3 cup finely minced onion
3 cloves garlic, minced
3 (10 oz. each) pkg. frozen chopped spinach, thawed and squeezed dry

2/3 cup pitted ripe olives, coarsely chopped
1/2 cup raisins
1/2 tsp. red pepper flakes
1 1/2 cups grated mozzarella cheese
Flaky Pastry, page 135 (optional)

Heat oil in a large sauté pan; sauté onions and garlic until soft but not brown. Stir in spinach, olives, raisins and red pepper flakes; cook over medium heat for 2 to 3 minutes. Spoon mixture into a pastry-lined 9 x 13 pan (or into a 9 x 13 pan lightly brushed with olive oil). Top with cheese and bake at 350° for about 25 minutes or until cheese is browned and bubbly.

ONION AND APPLE BAKE

Servings: 8-10

Onions and apples make an excellent flavor combination. This dish is especially good served with pork. It is also good with cooked pork or turkey, cut into small pieces, added to it.

6 large Bermuda onions, sliced
4 cups water
8-10 tart cooking apples (Pippin or Granny Smith), peeled, cored and sliced
2 tbs. ground cinnamon

4 tbs. sugar
4 tbs. butter
1 tsp. salt
½ tsp. pepper
4 tbs. butter
⅔ cup onion cooking water

Cook onion slices in water for 10 minutes. Drain and reserve liquid. In a greased 9 x 13 pan, alternate layers of onions and apples, ending with a layer of apples. Sprinkle apple layers with cinnamon and sugar and dot with butter. Sprinkle onion layers with salt and pepper and dot with butter. Add ⅔ cup onion cooking liquid. Bake at 250°, adding more liquid if necessary, for 1 hour and 30 minutes.

CHEESY VEGETABLE QUICHE

Servings: 8-10

Make this dish in the summer when squash and herbs are fresh and serve it with the ripest tomatoes you can find.

2 lbs. zucchini or yellow crooked
   neck squash or a combination
10 eggs, well beaten
3 cups grated Jack or Swiss cheese

2 tsp. fresh dill weed, minced
2 tsp. fresh basil, chopped
2 tsp. fresh oregano or tarragon
½ cup grated Parmesan cheese

Grate squash coarsely into a colander and let drain for 10 minutes. Press out as much liquid as possible. Combine squash with eggs, Jack cheese, dill, basil and oregano. Pour into a lightly greased 9 x 13 pan. Sprinkle Parmesan cheese over top and bake at 350° for 40 to 50 minutes or until quiche is set and edges are slightly brown. Serve with sliced tomatoes.

CHILIES RELLENOS CASSEROLE

Servings: 6-8

Chilies rellenos are a real Mexican treat. In this version, the frying is eliminated, but not the flavor.

2 cups half and half
4 eggs
⅔ cup flour
6 (4 oz. each) cans whole green chilies

1 lb. Jack cheese, grated
2 (8 oz. each) cans tomato sauce
½ cup chopped cilantro

Beat half and half with eggs and flour until mixture is smooth. Split open chilies and rinse away seeds. Drain them on paper towels. Reserve 1 cup grated cheese. In a lightly greased 9 x 13 pan, make alternate layers of chilies, cheese and egg mixture. Pour tomato sauce over top and sprinkle with reserved cheese. Bake at 375° for 1 hour. Sprinkle with chopped cilantro and serve hot.

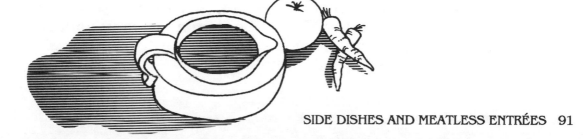

BAKED CHILI PUFF

Servings: 10-12

This is one of many variations on a theme. Chilies, cheese, eggs and milk are basic to all. They are perfect for brunch and also make a fine supper dish.

10 eggs
2 cups cottage cheese
½ cup butter or margarine, melted
1 lb. grated Jack or mozzarella cheese, or a combination
½ cup flour
1 tsp. baking powder
½ tsp. salt
2 (4 oz. each) cans whole green chilies, drained

Beat eggs until they are light. Beat in cottage cheese, butter, cheese, flour, baking powder and salt. Arrange chilies in a greased 9 x 13 baking dish. Pour egg mixture over and bake at 350° for about 30 minutes or until custard is set. Cool briefly before cutting into squares.

PRIENJAC

My friend Nan, who gave me this recipe, says it is pronounced pree-jan-yak.

1 (10 oz) pkg. frozen chopped
  spinach
6 eggs, beaten
8 tbs. butter or margarine, cut up

½ lb. sharp cheddar cheese, cut into
  ½-inch cubes
2 lbs. cottage cheese
6 tbs. flour

Defrost spinach and squeeze dry. Combine all ingredients in a bowl. Spoon into a greased 9 x 13 pan and bake at 350° for 1 hour or until top is browned. Cool to warm and cut into squares to serve.

VEGETABLE MELANGE WITH LENTILS

Servings: 10-12

This dish, which may be served as either a salad or a side dish, is even better after an overnight rest in the refrigerator.

2 cups uncooked lentils, rinsed and
  picked over
4 potatoes, peeled and diced
12 tomatoes, peeled, seeded and
  quartered
4 zucchini, sliced
12 green onions, sliced, including
  some green

4 stalks celery, sliced thin on the
  diagonal
4 onions, finely chopped
2 tbs. olive oil
6 cloves garlic, minced
½ cup chopped parsley
juice of 4 lemons

Boil lentils in water to cover for 45 minutes. Add potatoes, green onions and celery; simmer 15 minutes. Add more water, if needed. Add zucchini and tomatoes and simmer an additional 5 minutes. Don't add too much water, as mixture should be quite dry.

Sauté onion and garlic in oil until golden. Stir into vegetables and then gently stir in parsley and lemon juice. Spoon into a 9 x 13 serving dish and chill several hours or overnight. Bring to room temperature to serve.

BAKED VEGETABLE MEDLEY

Servings: 10-12

A fine dish for a summer supper or for a picnic. Serve it warm or at room temperature.

2 medium eggplants, peeled and
  cubed
4 zucchini, cubed
2 onions, chopped
1/2 cup olive oil
8 tomatoes, peeled, seeded and
  chopped

6 eggs
1 1/2 cups grated Parmesan cheese
2 tbs. minced parsley
1 tbs. chopped fresh basil
1 tsp. fresh oregano
salt and pepper
1/2 lb. mozzarella cheese, thinly sliced

Sauté eggplant, zucchini and onions in oil until softened, about 10 minutes. Add tomatoes; cover and simmer 20 to 25 minutes. Transfer to a bowl to cool. Beat eggs with Parmesan cheese, parsley, basil and oregano; combine with vegetables. Add salt and pepper to taste. Pour half the mixture into a greased 9 x 13 pan and top with 1/2 cup Parmesan cheese. Add remaining vegetables and Parmesan. Top all with mozzarella cheese. Bake at 350° for 45 to 50 minutes or until eggs are set and cheese is golden. Let cool before cutting into squares to serve.

PHYLLIS'S SCALLOPED MUSHROOMS

Servings: 10-12

This is not a dish for calorie counters, but don't pass it by unless you must. It's too good not to indulge in once in awhile. Make it ahead at least 1 hour.

1½ lbs. mushrooms, thickly sliced
1 (8 oz.) box Ritz crackers (3 stacks),
  crushed

1 cup heavy cream
¼ lb. butter or margarine, melted
salt and pepper

In a lightly buttered 9 x 13 pan, place ¾ of the mushrooms. Add ½ of the cracker crumbs, then remaining mushrooms and finally remaining crumbs. Pour cream evenly over contents of pan. When it has soaked in, top with melted butter. Salt and pepper top generously. Set aside for 1 hour. Bake at 350° for 30 minutes.

CAULIFLOWER-CHEESE BAKE

Servings: 8-10

When you are looking for something a bit unusual, turn to this recipe. It's a hearty vegetarian dish.

1½ cups beer
4 cups dark rye bread cubes
1 large or 2 small heads cauliflower, cut into bite-size florets
3 tbs. butter or margarine
1½ tsp. caraway seeds, lightly crushed

3½ cups grated sharp cheddar cheese
6 eggs
1½ tsp. dry mustard
1 tsp. ground coriander
pepper

At least an hour before you start cooking, pour beer into a bowl for it to become flat. Dry bread cubes on a baking sheet in a 300° oven until crisp. Sauté cauliflower in butter with caraway seeds until barely tender.

Combine cauliflower, bread and cheese; spoon it into a greased 9 x 13 pan. Mix together beer, eggs, mustard and coriander; pour over cauliflower. Bake at 350° for 30 to 45 minutes or until puffed and golden.

BLACK BEAN CHILI

Servings: 10-12

Black bean chili has become popular, and this vegetarian version is especially good. For a party it's fun to top it with a crispy corn bread crust.

2 tbs. vegetable oil
2 large onions, chopped
4 cloves garlic, chopped
1 tsp. cumin seeds
2 tsp. ground cumin
2-4 tbs. chili powder or to taste
salt and pepper

2 (28 oz. each) cans tomatoes,
   chopped and drained (reserve liquid)
1 cup chopped cilantro
3 cups dried black beans, cooked and
   drained
corn bread crust

Sauté onion and garlic in oil until soft but not brown. Add cumin, (seeds and ground), chili powder, salt, pepper, tomatoes, cilantro and beans. Add enough of reserved tomato liquid to make desired consistency. Simmer uncovered for 20 minutes, adding more tomato liquid as necessary. Spoon into a 9 x 13 pan. About 30 minutes before serving, top with corn bread crust and bake.

Corn Bread Crust

2 cups yellow cornmeal
2 cups flour
⅓ cup sugar
6 tbs. baking powder

1 tsp. salt
2 cups milk
½ cup melted butter or margarine

Preheat oven to 425°. Combine all ingredients and beat with a fork until batter is smooth. Spread mixture evenly over chili. Bake for about 30 minutes or until corn bread is golden and tests done. Serve immediately.

STUFFED RED AND YELLOW BELL PEPPERS DELUXE

Servings: 12

Get out your best and most flavorful olive oil for this dish. And splurge on red and yellow bell peppers. The exceptional results will make you glad you did not compromise.

1½ cups plus 4 tbs. olive oil
10 onions, minced
6 tbs. pine nuts
2 cups *uncooked* long grain rice
4 tomatoes, peeled, seeded and
   finely chopped
6 tbs. currants
2 tbs. sugar
6 tbs. fresh mint, minced
6 tbs. fresh dill, minced or 2 tbs. dried

1 tsp. ground cinnamon
¼ tsp. allspice
⅛ tsp. ground cloves
¼ tsp. grated nutmeg
salt
water
12 red and yellow bell peppers, tops
   and seeds removed
juice of 2 lemons

Heat olive oil and sauté onions and pine nuts for 20 minutes. Add rice and cook 15 minutes, stirring frequently. Add tomatoes and cook 5 minutes. Stir in currants, sugar, mint dill, cinnamon, allspice, cloves, nutmeg, salt and 1½ cups hot water. Stir well to blend, cover and simmer for 20 minutes or until all water is absorbed. Remove from heat and cool.

Stuff peppers firmly but not too tightly. Leave room for rice to expand. Spread a sheet of waxed paper in the bottom of a 9 x 13 pan. Place peppers on top of it. Combine 2 cups hot water with ½ tsp salt and 4 tbs. olive oil ; pour over peppers. Cover with foil and bake at 350° for 40 to 50 minutes or until peppers and rice are tender. Add hot water 2 or 3 tbs. at a time during baking, if needed. Most of the liquid should be gone when the peppers are done.

Cool peppers in pan and serve cold or at room temperature sprinkled with lemon juice.

TURKISH EGGPLANT

Servings: 6-8

In Turkey this is called Iman Baaldi. Regular eggplants are fine, but I like to use the small, longish Oriental variety and serve one per person.

3 small eggplants or 8 Oriental
  eggplants
olive oil
3 tomatoes, peeled, seeded and
  chopped
1 onion, chopped
1 cup pitted ripe olives, chopped

1 cup currants
1 tsp. ground cumin
2 tbs. curry powder
1 tsp. thyme
salt and pepper
1/2 cup chopped parsley
6-8 lemon wedges

Cut eggplants in half lengthwise and carefully remove most of the flesh without damaging skins. (A melon baller works well for this.) Chop flesh and sauté in smallest amount of olive oil as needed. Cook over medium heat for 15 minutes.

Fill a 9 x 13 pan with hot water to a depth of 1/4 inch, or less if using Oriental eggplants. Add 2 tbs. olive oil. Fill eggplant shells with tomato mixture and place them skin side down in pan. Bake at 300° for 1 1/2 to 2 hours (depending on size) or until skins are blackened slightly. Cool. Sprinkle with chopped parsley and serve with lemon wedges.

ARTICHOKE BOTTOMS WITH CHEESE SOUFFLÉS

This a truly elegant first course or side dish. As a first course, it will serve 6 to 8.

24 cooked artichoke bottoms
  (canned are fine)
4 tbs. butter or margarine
¾ cup chicken stock
4 tbs. butter
6 tbs. flour

1 cup milk
1⅓ cup grated cheese, a combination of Parmesan and Swiss
salt and pepper
6 eggs, separated

Melt 4 tbs. butter in a 9 x 13 pan. Add artichoke bottoms in a single layer and heat briefly. Add stock and simmer 1 minute. Set aside.

Melt remaining butter in a saucepan and whisk in flour. Cook 1 minute and slowly whisk in milk. Whisk until smooth. Stir in cheese, egg yolks, salt and pepper. Beat egg whites until they hold soft peaks. Fold them into cheese mixture and pile onto artichoke bottoms. Bake at 350° for about 20 minutes or until soufflés are puffed and golden. Serve immediately.

TOMATOES PROVENÇAL

Servings: 12-14

Serve these French-inspired tomatoes hot for a winter dinner or at room temperature for a summer brunch. They're delicious anytime.

8 large, firm but ripe tomatoes
3 cloves garlic, crushed
4 tbs. finely chopped onion
4 tbs. finely chopped parsley

1 tsp. dried basil or 2 tbs. fresh,
  minced
salt and pepper
½ cup dry bread crumbs
olive oil

Cut tomatoes in half crosswise. Arrange them cut side up in a lightly oiled 9 x 13 pan. Combine garlic, onion, parsley, basil, salt and pepper with bread crumbs. Stir in enough olive oil to make a paste. Spread mixture on tomato halves and broil 3 inches from heat for about 10 minutes or until topping is nicely browned. Watch carefully to avoid burning.

GREEN TOMATO PARMIGIANA

If you've every wondered what to do with all the green tomatoes at the end of the summer, here is one tasty answer.

½ cup plus 1 tbs. olive oil
⅓ cup chopped onion
2 cloves garlic, minced
3 (8 oz. each) cans tomato sauce
1 tbs. chopped parsley
salt and pepper

1 large egg
⅓ cup milk
8 medium green tomatoes
½ cup flour
⅔ cup grated mozzarella cheese
⅔ cup grated Parmesan cheese

Heat ¼ cup oil and add onion and garlic. Sauté 5 minutes. Stir in tomato sauce, parsley, salt and pepper; simmer uncovered for 30 minutes. In a small dish, beat together egg, milk and 1 tbs. oil. Slice tomatoes into ½-inch slices; first coat each slice with flour and then dip into egg mixture. Heat ¼ cup oil in a skillet and fry tomato slices until golden on each side. Cover bottom of a 9 x 13 pan with tomato sauce. Add a layer of fried tomatoes and a layer of cheeses. Bake at 350° for 30-35 minutes or until bubbly. Serve immediately.

BAKED FENNEL WITH CHEESE

Servings: 8-10

Fennel is a celery-like vegetable with a delicate anise flavor. Beloved by Italians, who call it finoccio, it is often overlooked here. It's available from fall through spring and when baked, as in this dish, the anise flavor becomes elusive.

6 medium fennel bulbs
6 cups beef stock
¾ cup dry white wine
salt and pepper

10 tbs. butter or margarine
⅔ cup grated Swiss cheese
⅔ cup grated Fontina cheese
⅓ cup grated Parmesan cheese

Wash, dry and trim fennel bulbs, discarding feathery stalks. Cut each bulb in half lengthwise and place in a large sauté pan. Cover with stock and wine; simmer gently, uncovered, for 15 minutes or until fennel is tender but still firm. Drain. Place fennel, cut side up, in a lightly oiled 9 x 13 pan. Sprinkle with salt and pepper and dot with butter. Combine cheeses and sprinkle over fennel. Bake, uncovered, at 350° for 10 to 12 minutes or until cheese is bubbly.

WILD RICE-MUSHROOM CASSEROLE

Servings 8-10

The earthy flavors of wild rice and mushrooms combine well. My original recipe calls for white button mushrooms, but do not hesitate to substitute one of the wild (but now cultivated) varieties for a special treat.

1½ cup uncooked wild rice
1½ tsp. salt
¾ lb. mushrooms, thickly sliced
3 tbs. butter or margarine
6 slices bacon, finely chopped
2½ cups thinly sliced celery

2 large onions, chopped
1 large green bell pepper, seeded and chopped
7 tbs. full-flavored olive oil
¾ cup tomato juice

Cook rice until tender (about 20 minutes) in boiling water to cover. Drain thoroughly and spoon into a greased 9 x 13 pan. Sauté mushrooms in butter for 3 to 4 minutes. In another pan, fry chopped bacon until it is crisp. Add celery, onions and green pepper; sauté until vegetables are soft. Stir in mushrooms, including pan juices, olive oil and tomato juice. Pour over wild rice. Bake at 350° until liquid is absorbed, about 30 minutes.

CON QUESO RICE

Servings: 8-10

Rice and beans are a favorite combination in much of Latin America. Black beans are especially flavorful.

3 cloves garlic, minced
1 onion, chopped
2 tbs. vegetable oil
½ lb. ricotta cheese
½ cup milk
3 cups grated Jack or cheddar
  cheese

1 (4 oz.) can chopped green chilies
3 cups cooked brown rice
1½ cups cooked black beans
½ cup grated Jack or cheddar
  cheese

Sauté garlic and onion in oil. Mix ricotta cheese with milk and Jack cheese. Combine rice, beans, garlic, onion and chilies. Layer rice/bean mixture in a greased 9 x 13 pan with cheese mixture, ending with cheese mixture. Bake at 350° for 30 minutes. Sprinkle with remaining cheese and bake for 5 minutes longer.

BAKED BULGAR BALKAN STYLE

Servings: 10-12

This is an out-of-the-ordinary dish to serve with meat or chicken.

4 cups green bell pepper, seeded
  and finely chopped
2 cups onion, finely chopped
2 cups mushrooms, sliced
3-4 tbs. butter or margarine
3 tbs. tamari sauce
2 tbs. dry sherry
1½ tsp. marjoram

salt and pepper
2 cups uncooked bulgar soaked in
  2 cups boiling water for 15 to
  20 minutes
2 cups cottage cheese
1 cup feta cheese, crumbled
6 eggs, beaten

Sauté green pepper, onions and mushrooms in butter until vegetables are soft. Add tamari, sherry, marjoram, salt and pepper. Combine cottage cheese and feta cheese. Spread bulgar in an oiled 9 x 13 pan. Top with vegetables. Top with cheeses. Pour beaten eggs over all. Bake at 350° for 45 minutes. Let stand 15 minutes before serving.

BAR COOKIES

BEST BROWNIES

24 squares

These are the best. The recipe comes from a dear friend of long standing who says, "They taste like fudge," and so they do. I sometimes add a cup of coarsely chopped nuts because that's the way I like my brownies — and my fudge.

4 (1 oz. each) squares unsweetened
  chocolate
½ cup butter or margarine
4 eggs
2 cups sugar

¼ tsp. salt
½ tsp. vanilla
1 cup flour
1 cup nuts, coarsely chopped
  (optional)

In a saucepan, melt chocolate and butter over low heat. Watch carefully and do not burn chocolate. Set aside to cool. Beat together eggs, sugar, salt and vanilla. Stir in chocolate mixture and then flour; combine well. Spoon into a lightly buttered 9 x 13 pan and bake at 350° for 30 minutes. Cool in pan on a wire rack before cutting into squares.

FUDGE CRISPIES

This thin fudgy cookies are quickly prepared, and disappear just about as quickly.

2 (1 oz. each) squares unsweetened
  chocolate
½ cup butter or margarine
½ cup flour
¾ cup sugar

¼ tsp. salt
2 eggs, well beaten
1 tsp. vanilla
1 cup finely chopped nuts

In a saucepan, melt chocolate and butter over low heat. Watch carefully and do not burn chocolate. Combine flour, sugar and salt; add to chocolate mixture. Remove from heat and stir well. Stir in eggs and vanilla, and finally nuts. Spread in a buttered 9 x 13 pan and bake at 400° for 12 to 15 minutes. Cool in pan on a wire rack and cut into squares when cool.

LEMON SQUARES

This is an old favorite, almost a classic. Sinfully rich and sinfully good, they should be cut into small squares. They pair especially well with fresh berries or peaches.

2 cups flour
1 cup butter or margarine, softened
½ cup powdered sugar
4 eggs, beaten

1½ cups granulated sugar
6 tbs. lemon juice
4 tbs. flour
1 tsp. baking powder

Combine flour, butter and powdered sugar with fingers until mixture is crumbly. Press it into a 9 x 13 pan and bake at 350° for 12 to 15 minutes or until golden. Combine beaten eggs, sugar and lemon juice; beat for several minutes. Sift in flour and baking powder and stir to combine. Pour this mixture over baked layer and continue to bake at 350° for 20 minutes or until top is golden. Let cool in pan and cut into squares.

PERSIMMON BARS WITH LEMON GLAZE

24 squares

These spicy bars will keep well and can be made from either fresh or frozen persimmon puree. Don't be tempted to skip the glaze, because its tartness is a nice contrast to the sweet persimmon.

1 cup persimmon puree (add 1½ tsp. lemon juice to fresh puree)
1 tsp. baking soda
1 egg
1 cup sugar
½ cup vegetable oil

1 cup pitted dates, cut into small pieces
1¾ cups flour
1 tsp. *each* salt, ground cinnamon and grated nutmeg
½ tsp. ground cloves
1 cup chopped pecans

Mix persimmon puree with soda and set aside. In a bowl, combine egg, sugar, oil and dates; mix well. Combine flour, salt, cinnamon, nutmeg and cloves. Add to date mixture alternately with persimmon puree. Mix just enough to blend. Stir in nuts and spread in a buttered and floured 9 x 13 pan. Bake at 350° for about 35 minutes or until slightly browned. Cool in pan on a wire rack for 5 minutes; spread with *Lemon Glaze*. Cool completely and cut into bars.

Lemon Glaze

Blend 1 cup unsifted powdered sugar with 2 tbs. lemon juice until smooth.

MINCEMEAT-OAT BARS

These flavorful bars pack well in a lunch box or are a just-right accompaniment to a cup of coffee or tea. Cut into larger than cookie-size squares and topped with a scoop of vanilla ice cream, they become a fit-for-company dessert.

2½ cups flour
2 cups quick cooking rolled oats
1½ cups brown sugar, packed
½ tsp. salt
1 cup butter or margarine, softened

1 jar (1 lb. 12 oz.) prepared mincemeat
½ cup walnuts, chopped
3 tbs. rum, brandy or orange juice
3 tbs. milk, about

Combine flour, oats, sugar and salt. With a pastry blender or fingers, cut in butter until it makes a coarse crumb. Spread half of the mixture evenly over bottom of an unbuttered 9 x 13 pan and press gently into place. Combine mincemeat with nuts and spread evenly over crumb mixture. Sprinkle remaining crumbs over top and press it lightly with a fork. Dip a pastry brush in milk and lightly moisten surface. Bake at 400° for 25 to 30 minutes or until lightly browned. Cool in pan on a wire rack and cut into squares when cool.

WALNUT BUTTER COOKIES

24 squares

These rich cookies are all-time favorites of mine and are always included in my Christmas baking. In this recipe, real butter makes a big difference. I use the unsalted variety.

1 cup butter, softened
1 cup sugar
1 egg yolk

2 cups flour
1 tsp. vanilla
1¼ cups finely chopped walnuts

Cream butter and sugar until fluffy. Add egg yolk and mix well. Add flour and vanilla and mix well. Mix in nuts. Press dough evenly into an unbuttered 9 x 13 pan. Bake at 350° for 20 to 25 minutes or until just lightly browned. Cool slightly in pan on a wire rack and cut into squares while still warm.

ALMOND-DATE BARS

*Dates, almonds and chocolate compliment one another in this flavorful Ukrainian treat. Save the extra egg yolks for **Golden Cake**, page 130.*

1 cup flour	½ tsp. vanilla
2 tbs. sugar	6 egg whites
pinch of salt	2 cups powdered sugar
¼ cup butter or margarine, softened	1 cup almonds, finely chopped
2 egg yolks	1 cup pitted dates, finely chopped
1 tbs. heavy cream	1 cup grated semi-sweet chocolate

Combine flour, sugar and salt. With a pastry blender or fingers, cut in butter until it makes a coarse crumb. Beat together egg yolks, cream and vanilla; add them to flour mixture. Mix until dough leaves sides of bowl and then press evenly into a well-buttered 9 x 13 pan. Bake at 350° for 10 to 15 minutes.

While dough is baking, beat egg whites until frothy. Add powdered sugar and beat to a stiff meringue. Fold in almonds, dates and chocolate. Spread over partially baked shell and continue to bake for 40 minutes or until meringue is set. Cool in pan on a wire rack and cut into squares when cool.

MOTHER'S CHOCOLATE CHIP BARS

24 squares

This recipe from my mother's files is yet another version of the all-American chocolate chip cookie.

½ cup butter or margarine, softened
½ cup shortening
½ cup brown sugar, packed
½ cup white sugar

2 egg yolks
2 cups flour
½ tsp. salt
1 tsp. baking powder

Topping
1 (12 oz.) pkg. chocolate chips
2 egg whites

1 cup brown sugar, packed
1 tsp. vanilla

Cream butter and sugar until fluffy. Add egg yolks and blend well. Combine flour, salt and baking powder and blend into creamed mixture. Press dough evenly into an unbuttered 9 x 13 pan. Sprinkle chocolate chips over. Beat egg whites until they hold soft peaks. Gradually beat in brown sugar and vanilla. Carefully spread meringue over chips. Bake at 350° for 25 minutes. Cool in pan on a wire rack. Cut into squares when cool.

CHOCOLATE CHIP COOKIE BRITTLE

1½ lbs.

These crisp cookies are easy to prepare and keep well either frozen or in an air-tight tin. They are an unusual change from the regular chocolate chip cookie.

1 cup butter or margarine, softened
1½ tsp. vanilla
1 tsp. salt
1 cup sugar

2 cups flour
½ cup finely chopped nuts
1 (6 oz.) pkg. chocolate chips

In a bowl, combine butter, vanilla and salt. Gradually beat in sugar. Add flour, nuts and chocolate chips; mix well. Press dough evenly into an unbuttered 9 x 13 pan and bake at 375° for 15 to 20 minutes. Watch carefully and remove from oven just when top turns golden. Cool in pan on a wire rack. Break cookies into irregular pieces and drain on absorbent paper.

DALE'S APRICOT SQUARES

24 squares

Another sweet treat from another dear friend of long standing. She says they are always a hit and I can vouch for that. Try making them with other flavors of jam or, for a change, marmalade is delicious.

1 cup sugar
¾ cup butter or margarine, softened
1 egg
½ tsp. vanilla
2 cups flour

½ tsp. salt
1½ cup shredded coconut (optional)
1 (12 oz.) jar apricot jam
½ cup chopped pecans

Cream sugar and butter until fluffy. Add egg and vanilla; mix well. Add flour and salt; mix well. Mix in coconut if desired. Press ¾ of the dough into a lightly buttered 9 x 13 pan. Spread with jam and sprinkle with nuts. Crumble remaining dough over top. Bake at 350° for 35 to 40 minutes. Cool in pan on a wire rack. Cut into squares when cool.

DATE-NUT BARS

These bars are easily made with an electric mixer, but I have often put them together without one. Dress them up with sifted powdered sugar after they cool, or serve them with ice cream. They are very thin.

¾ cup flour
1 tsp. baking powder
¼ tsp. salt
4 egg whites, at room temperature
1 whole egg, at room temperature
¾ cup sugar
1 cup chopped and pitted dates
½ cup finely chopped pecans

Combine flour, baking powder and salt; set aside. In a large bowl, beat egg whites and whole egg until mixture is thick. Stir in dry ingredients, dates and nuts. Pour batter into a buttered 9 x 13 pan and bake at 300° about 25 minutes or until it feels springy and tests done. Cool slightly and cut into squares.

PECAN CRUNCHIES

These versatile cookies can be served alone or topped with whipped cream or ice cream for a special dessert.

1 cup butter or margarine
1 cup sugar
2 cups flour
2 tsp. ground cinnamon
1 egg, separated
½ cup sugar
2 tbs. ground cinnamon
1 cup finely chopped pecans

Cream butter and 1 cup sugar until fluffy. Add flour and 2 tsp. cinnamon; mix well. Stir in egg yolk and mix well. Press dough into a well-buttered 9 x 13 pan. Beat egg white until it is foamy and brush it over surface. Combine ½ cup sugar, 2 tbs. cinnamon and pecans; sprinkle evenly over egg white. Bake at 350° for 25 to 30 minutes. Cut into squares or bars while warm, but cool in pan on a wire rack.

CAKES, PIES AND DESSERTS

JOYCE'S OATMEAL CAKE

Servings: 10-12

A simple cake, and always good. Other dried fruits, or a combination of several, may be substituted for the dates or raisins.

1½ cups boiling water
1 cup quick cooking oats
1 cup brown sugar, packed
1 cup white sugar
½ cup butter or margarine
1 tsp. vanilla
2 eggs, beaten

1½ cups flour
½ tsp. salt
1 tsp. baking soda
1 tsp. baking powder
1 tsp. ground cinnamon
1 cup chopped dates or raisins

Pour water over oats and let stand. Cream sugars with butter until fluffy. Add vanilla and egg; mix well. Combine flour, salt, soda, baking powder and cinnamon; add to creamed mixture. Stir in dates. Add oatmeal and water. Batter will be quite thick. Spoon it into a buttered 9 x 13 pan and bake at 350° for 35 to 40 minutes or until it tests done. Cool in pan on a wire rack.

Broiled Topping

⅔ cup chopped nuts
⅔ cup flaked coconut
1 cup brown sugar, packed
2 tbs. butter or margarine
3 tbs. milk or cream

Combine all topping ingredients in a saucepan over low heat just to melt sugar and butter. Do not cook. Spread on baked cake and place under the broiler, about 4 inches from heat, until brown and bubbly.

NANCY'S CHOCOLATE APPLESAUCE CAKE

Servings: 10-12

This rich, moist cake is a perfect traveler, just right to take along when you are asked to bring the dessert. If you toast the nuts before adding them to the batter, the final result will be extra good.

2 cups flour
2 tsp. baking soda
1 tsp. baking power
½ tsp. salt
½ tsp. grated nutmeg
½ tsp. allspice
¼ tsp. ground cloves
1 tsp. ground cinnamon

⅓ cup ground unsweetened chocolate
1 egg
1 cup sugar
½ cup vegetable oil
2 cups unsweetened applesauce
1 cup raisins
1 cup finely chopped nuts

Combine flour, soda, baking powder, salt, nutmeg, allspice, cloves, cinnamon and chocolate; mix with a wire whisk. In another bowl, combine egg, sugar, oil and applesauce; add this to the dry mixture. Combine well. Stir in raisins and nuts; mix well. Spoon batter into a buttered and floured 9 x 13 pan and bake at 350° for 30 to 35 minutes or until it tests done. Cool in pan on a wire rack.

OLIVE-PINEAPPLE CAKE

The unusual ingredients in this cake create a wonderfully elusive flavor. It's very moist and needs no frosting. Here's a recipe in which California ripe olives, rather than imported, are best.

2 cups sugar
1½ cups olive oil
1½ cups chopped California ripe
 olives
4 eggs
1 (8½ oz.) can crushed pineapple,
 drained

2 cups flour
2 tsp. baking soda
2 tsp. ground cinnamon
1½ tsp. baking powder
½ cup chopped walnuts

Combine sugar, oil, olives, eggs and pineapple; mix well. In another bowl, combine flour, baking powder, cinnamon, soda and walnuts; mix well. Add dry mixture to olive mixture and mix well. Spoon batter into a buttered and floured 9 x 13 pan and bake at 350° for 40 to 45 minutes or until the cake tests done. Cool in pan on a wire rack.

MOTHER'S MOIST BANANA CAKE

Servings: 10-12

This is a very simple, old-fashioned cake which always tastes wonderful. Mash the bananas with a fork and leave a few lumps for texture.

2 cups flour
1 tsp. baking soda
¼ tsp. salt
½ cup butter or margarine, softened
1½ cups sugar

2 eggs, beaten
1½ cups mashed banana (4 or 5 bananas)
1 tsp. vanilla
½ cup sour milk or buttermilk

Combine flour, baking soda and salt. In another bowl, cream butter and sugar until fluffy. Add eggs, bananas and vanilla to creamed mixture. Add flour alternately with sour milk. Mix thoroughly. Spoon batter into a buttered 9 x 13 pan and bake at 350° for 45 minutes or until the cake tests done. Cool in pan on a wire rack.

CRANBERRY-APPLE CAKE

Servings: 10-12

This cake is not very sweet. Serve it for a breakfast treat or as a snack with coffee or tea. It does require a blender or food processor.

1 cup honey
2 tbs. orange juice concentrate,
  undiluted
½ cup vegetable oil
2 eggs
2 cups flour
1 tsp. baking soda

1½ tsp. ground cinnamon
½ tsp. grated nutmeg
1½ tsp. vanilla
2 cups coarsely chopped and peeled
  apples
2 cups coarsely chopped cranberries
¾ cup coarsely chopped walnuts

Mix honey and orange juice concentrate in a blender or food processor for 10 minutes. Remove to a bowl and add oil. Add eggs and vanilla; mix well. Combine flour, soda, cinnamon and nutmeg; add to honey mixture. Combine thoroughly and then fold in apples, cranberries and nuts. Spoon into a well-buttered 9 x 13 pan and bake at 350° for 45 to 50 minutes or until cake tests done. Cool in pan on a wire rack.

GOLDEN CAKE

Servings: 10-12

This light textured yellow cake is a good excuse to use up extra egg yolks. Try substituting other flavors for the orange extract for a change. Frost or not, as you choose.

4 cups cake flour
6 tsp. baking powder
1 cup butter or margarine, softened
2 cups sugar

6 egg yolks, beaten until thick
1½ cups milk
1 tsp. orange extract

Combine flour and baking powder; stir with a wire whisk. In another bowl, cream butter and sugar until fluffy. Add beaten egg yolks and combine well. Add flour alternately with milk. Add extract and beat well. Pour batter into a well-buttered 9 x 13 pan and bake at 350° for about an hour or until cake tests done. Cool in pan on a wire rack.

PERSIMMON CAKE WITH BROWN SAUCE Servings: 10-12

Two ripe persimmons will equal about 2 cups of puree. No need to peel. Just remove the stems and whir in a food processor or blender until smooth.

2 cups persimmon puree
2 cups sugar
2 eggs, beaten
1 cup milk
½ tsp. lemon juice
½ tsp. vanilla

2 cups flour
1 tbs. baking soda
2 tsp. ground cinnamon
2 tbs. butter or margarine, melted
1 cup chopped nuts
1 cup raisins

Combine persimmon puree and eggs; set aside. Add lemon juice and vanilla to milk. Combine flour, soda and cinnamon; add them to persimmon mixture alternately with milk. Stir just enough to combine. Mix in melted butter, nuts and raisins. Spoon batter into a buttered 9 x 13 pan. Bake at 350° for 1 hour and serve warm with *Brown Sauce*.

Brown Sauce

1½ cups brown sugar, packed
3 tbs. flour

8 tbs. butter or margarine
1½ cups boiling water

Combine sugar and flour in a saucepan. Cut in butter. Pour in boiling water and heat slowly, stirring constantly until sauce boils and thickens.

FRESH APPLE CAKE

Servings: 10-12

This cake is as easy to prepare as it is good to eat, and my spattered recipe card testifies to many years of use. In fact, it's a cake my children used to make for themselves after school. Of course, it was always gone before dinner.

4 cups peeled and sliced apples
2 eggs
½ cup vegetable oil
2 cups sugar
2 cups flour

2 tsp. baking soda
2 tsp. ground cinnamon
1 tsp. salt
1½ cups chopped walnuts

In a large bowl, combine apples and eggs. Add oil and sugar; mix well. Combine flour, soda, cinnamon and salt; add to apple mixture. Stir in nuts. Spoon batter into a buttered 9 x 13 pan and bake at 350° for 40 minutes or until cake tests done. Cool in pan on a wire rack.

GINGERBREAD WITH LEMON SAUCE

Servings: 10-12

There is something comforting about good gingerbread, and this moist version is especially good. Serve it warm with Lemon Sauce.

4 eggs, beaten
1 cup sour cream
1 cup molasses
1 cup brown sugar, packed

3 cups flour
2 tsp. baking soda
2 tsp. ground ginger
1 cup melted butter or margarine

Combine beaten eggs with sour cream, molasses and brown sugar; beat well. Combine flour, soda and ginger; stir into egg mixture. Add butter and beat well. Spoon into a buttered 9 x 13 pan and bake at 350° for 30 minutes or until cake tests done. Cool briefly in pan on a wire rack; serve warm with *Lemon Sauce*.

Lemon Sauce

1 cup sugar
4 tbs. cornstarch
2 cups water
4 tbs. butter or margarine

2 tbs. lemon juice
2 tsp. grated lemon peel
12 regular size marshmallows,
  snipped into small pieces

Combine sugar and cornstarch with water in the top of a double boiler over simmering water. Cook, stirring until transparent. Then add remaining ingredients and mix with a wire whisk until smooth. Serve hot.

FRESH PEACH PIE

Servings: 10-12

This luscious pie can be baked as a one crust, 9-inch pie (use half the recipe), but if you need an especially good dessert for a crowd during fresh peach season, here's the answer. Use the Flaky Pastry below or your favorite pie crust.

Flaky Pastry (for 1 crust in a 9 x 13 pan)
2½ cups flour
½ tsp. salt
½ cup cold butter, margarine or solid shortening (or a combination)
¼ cup ice water, about

Mix flour and salt. Cut in butter until mixture resembles coarse meal. Add water slowly and stir with a fork. Add only enough water for dough to form a ball. Wrap dough in plastic wrap and refrigerate for 15 minutes before rolling on a floured board.

Filling

10 cups peeled, sliced fresh peaches
6 tbs. lemon juice
⅔ cup sugar
6 tbs. cornstarch

1 cup sugar
6 tbs. butter, cut in small pieces
1 tsp. almond extract
whipped cream or ice cream

Line a 9 x 13 baking dish with pastry. Cover it with foil and a layer of dried beans or pie weights. Bake at 425° for 10 to 12 minutes or until sides are lightly browned. Remove foil and beans; continue to bake for 2 minutes. Set aside to cool.

Place peach slices in a bowl with lemon juice and ⅔ cup sugar. Stir gently and let stand 1 hour. Stir once or twice.

In a saucepan, combine cornstarch and 1 cup sugar. Drain juice that has accumulated from peach slices and add enough water to make 3 cups. Stir this into cornstarch and sugar; cook over low heat until sauce thickens. Remove from heat and add butter and almond extract. Gently stir sauce into peaches. You may not need it all, just enough to make a nice balance between peaches and sauce. Pour peaches into baked shell and refrigerate. Cut in squares to serve.

CLAFOUTIS

Servings: 10-12

A clafouti is a country fresh dessert of fresh fruit and an eggy batter. There are many variations. Cherries are traditional, but peaches, plums, apricots, pears or a combination of these all make a delightful dessert. Two versions follow. The first is a fruit-filled custard. The second is a fruit-filled cake.

Clafouti I

1 lb. fresh fruit (cherries, plums,
   apricots, pears or a combination)
4 whole eggs
2 egg yolks
3 tbs. sugar

2 cups milk
4 tbs. kirsch or ½ tsp. vanilla
sugar

Remove pits from fruit. Cut plums and apricots into pieces. Peel pears, remove cores and cut in pieces. Arrange fruit in a buttered 9 x 13 baking dish.

Beat whole eggs, egg yolks and sugar together. Then beat in milk and kirsch. Strain this custard over fruit and bake at 325° for 45 to 60 minutes or until browned on top and set. Serve warm sprinkled with sugar.

Clafouti II

6 peaches, peeled, pitted and cut into slices
½ cup sugar
⅓ cup amaretto or kirsch
2 egg yolks
4 whole eggs
1 cup sugar

1 cup butter or margarine, softened
2 cups flour
2 cups milk
½ tsp. almond or vanilla extract
½ cup sliced, toasted almonds
powdered sugar

Combine sugar and amaretto. Add peach slices and marinate for 30 minutes. Combine egg yolks, whole eggs and sugar; beat *well*. Add butter and flour; mix well. Butter a 9 x 13 baking dish. Lay peach slices in dish. Sprinkle with almonds. Cover with batter. Bake at 375° for about 45 minutes or until it is puffed and browned. Sprinkle with powdered sugar and serve warm.

CANDY APPLE PIE

This dessert goes together quickly and easily, and it's always a hit. Serve it with whipped or ice cream.

8 apples, peeled, cored and sliced
½ cup sugar
1 tsp. ground cinnamon
1 cup brown sugar, packed

½ cup butter or margarine, softened
¾ cup flour
¾ cup quick cooking rolled oats

Place apples in a buttered 9 x 13 pan and sprinkle with sugar and cinnamon. In a bowl, blend together brown sugar, butter, flour and oats. Pat it down on top of apples. It may not cover completely. Bake at 400° for 30 minutes. Serve warm.

DRIED FRUIT COBBLER

Servings: 10-12

This is what I think of as a "comforting food." It's a not-too-sweet, simple dessert filled with fruit and is delicious served warm or cold. The variety of fruit is up to you, but try to include both sweet and tart. Some people like this cobbler with sour cream, but a scoop of vanilla ice cream is my choice.

3 cups mixed dried fruit
4 cups water
1½ cups sugar
2 tbs. lemon juice
½ tsp. allspice
1 cup sugar

½ cup butter or margarine, softened
2 cups flour
3 tsp. baking powder
¼ tsp. salt
1 cup milk
powdered sugar

With scissors, snip fruit into small pieces. In a saucepan, combine fruit, water, 1½ cups sugar, lemon juice and allspice. Bring to a boil and simmer for 10 minutes. Cream together 1 cup sugar and butter. Mix baking powder and salt with flour. Add dry mixture alternately with milk to creamed mixture. Butter a 9 x 13 baking dish and spread batter in it. Spoon fruits and their liquid over batter and bake at 375° for 30 to 35 minutes or until cake tests done. Serve warm or cold dusted with powdered sugar.

PHYLLIS'S FRENCH APPLE TORTE

Servings: 10-12

This recipe makes a thin and delicious torte in the French manner. Serve it with sherry-laced whipped cream, if desired, but it needs little embellishment.

⅓ cup flour
2½ tsp. baking powder
½ tsp. salt
3 eggs, beaten
1¼ cups sugar

½ tsp. vanilla
1 cup chopped walnuts or pecans
1½ cups peeled and chopped apples
powdered sugar

With a whisk, combine flour, baking powder and salt in a bowl. In another bowl, mix eggs, sugar and vanilla; add them to flour mixture. Combine well. Fold in nuts and apples; spoon batter into a buttered 9 x 13 baking dish. Bake at 350° for 35 minutes. Cool in dish on a wire rack and sprinkle with powdered sugar before serving.

CHOCOLATE PIE IN GRANOLA CRUST

Servings: 10-12

This heavenly rich chocolate pie is complimented by the crunchy granola crust.

4 cups granola, crushed to remove lumps
½ cup butter or margarine, melted
⅔ cup finely chopped nuts
1 (12 oz.) pkg. semisweet chocolate chips

6 tbs. milk
4 tbs. sugar
8 eggs, separated
2 tsp. vanilla
2 cups heavy cream

Combine granola, melted butter and nuts; mix well. Press mixture firmly into the bottom of a buttered 9 x 13 baking dish and bake at 350° for 15 minutes. Cool.

In a double boiler over simmering water, combine chocolate chips, milk and sugar. Whisk as chocolate melts. Remove from heat and, when cool, add egg yolks, one at a time, whisking hard after each addition. Stir in vanilla. Beat egg whites until they hold stiff peaks. Mix about ⅓ of them into chocolate mixture and then fold in remaining ⅔. Beat 1 cup of cream until it holds soft peaks and fold it into chocolate mixture. Pour into prepared shell, cover and refrigerate several hours or overnight. Just before serving, beat remaining 1 cup of cream and spread it over the top. Dust with grated chocolate if desired.

NESSELRODE PIE IN COOKIE CRUMB CRUST

Servings: 10-12

Count Nesselrode was a 19th Century Russian bon vivant after whom a creamy, enriched pudding was named. This is one royal version.

4 cups crushed vanilla wafer crumbs
½ cup butter, melted
4 tbs. rum
3 envelopes (3 tbs.) plain gelatin
1½ cups cold water
4 cups half and half

4 eggs, separated
½ cup sugar
3 tbs. rum
¾ cups sugar
bittersweet chocolate

Combine crumbs, butter and 4 tbs. rum; mix well. Press firmly into a 9 x 13 baking dish and bake at 350° for 15 minutes. Set aside to cool. Soften gelatin in cold water and set aside. In a double boiler over simmering water, heat half and half. Beat egg yolks with ½ cup sugar and slowly whisk them into cream. Cook until mixture begins to thicken. Add gelatin and whisk to dissolve completely. Remove from heat and cool. Beat egg whites with run and ¾ cup sugar until they hold soft peaks. Stir a large spoonful into custard and then fold in remaining. Pour on top of crumb crust, cover and chill several hours or overnight. Garnish with grated bittersweet chocolate. Cut into squares to serve.

BAKED APPLES SUPREME

Servings: 8

I first tasted these at the home of a friend and I knew at once that I was eating no ordinary baked apples. For variety, add a few raisins and/or chopped nuts to the filling.

4 large baking apples (Golden
  Delicious or Fuji) cut across in half
⅓ cup sugar, scant
grated peel of 2 lemons
2 Pippin or Granny Smith apples,
 peeled, cored and grated

4 tbs. heavy cream
2 egg yolks
¼ tsp. ground cinnamon
2 tbs. butter or margarine, cut into
  small pieces

Remove cores from baking apples and make a cavity to hold filling. (A small melon baller works well for this.) Place apples, cut side up, in a buttered 9 x 13 baking dish and sprinkle with 6 tbs. sugar. Pour ¼ cup water into dish and bake apples at 400° for 10 minutes.

Combine lemon peel, grated apple, 2 tbs. sugar, cream, egg yolks and cinnamon; fill apple cavities with this mixture. Dot with butter and continue to bake at 400° for 15 to 20 minutes or until apples are tender and tops golden. Serve warm or cold.

OVEN POACHED PEARS

Servings: 6

Poached pears are a wonderful fall and winter dessert. There are many variations, two of which are given here. Be sure to choose pears that are ripe but still firm.

6 Bosc, Bartlett or Red Mountain
  pears, peeled, halved and cored
2 cups port or dry red wine

½ cup honey
6 tbs. ricotta cheese

Cut a thin slice off the rounded half of the pear and arrange halves, cored side up, in a 9 x 13 pan. Combine port and honey and blend well. Spoon it over pears and bake at 375° for about 45 minutes. Baste several times.

To serve, place a rounded spoonful of ricotta cheese in each pear half. Spoon some pan syrup over cheese and pears; serve chilled or at room temperature.

Variation

6 Bosc, Bartlett or Red Mountain
  pears, peeled, halved and cored
1 cup sugar
2 cups water
4 tbs. raspberry vinegar

6 tbs. Saga blue or Gorgonzola
  cheese
½ cup coarsely chopped and toasted
  walnuts

Prepare pears as in recipe for *Oven Poached Pears*. Arrange in a 9 x 13 pan. In a saucepan, combine sugar, water and vinegar; bring to a boil. Pour hot syrup over pears and bake at 375° for 45 minutes, basting several times. Place a spoonful of cheese in each pear half and sprinkle with walnuts. Serve warm or cold topped with a spoonful or two of pan syrup.

MOTHER'S FROZEN DESSERT

Servings: 8-12

This is a good dessert to have "on hand" on the freezer. Choose any ice cream flavor that compliments chocolate. Peppermint, raspberry, mocha and vanilla are all good choices. Prepare wafers easily and without any mess by placing them in a plastic bag before crushing them with a rolling pin.

1 cup crushed vanilla wafers
⅔ cup butter or margarine
2 cups powdered sugar, sifted
3 eggs, separated

3 (1 oz. each) squares unsweetened
  chocolate
1 tsp. vanilla
1 qt. ice cream, softened

Line the bottom of a 9 x 13 pan with crushed wafers. Cream butter and sugar until fluffy. Add egg yolks and beat until smooth. Melt chocolate and add it to creamed mixture along with vanilla.

Beat egg whites until they hold soft peaks; fold them into chocolate mixture. Pour into crumb-lined pan and freeze for 3 hours. Then spread with softened ice cream. Wrap air tight and return to freezer. Cut into squares to serve.

GRANOLA-APPLE SQUARES

12 squares

This granola-topped apple pastry is a perfect dessert for a large informal gathering.

2 cups flour
2/3 cup sugar
3/4 cup butter or margarine, softened
2 egg yolks
6 apples, peeled and sliced
1½ cups granola, slightly crushed to remove lumps
½ cup coarsely chopped almonds or pecans
1 cup powdered sugar
3 tbs. lemon juice

Combine flour at ¼ cup sugar. Add butter and mix with fingers to form a coarse crumb. Stir in egg yolks and work dough with hands. When it forms a ball, press it evenly in the bottom of an unbuttered 9 x 13 pan.

Arrange apple slices on top. Mix granola with remaining granulated sugar and nuts; sprinkle over apples. Bake at 350° for about 1 hour or until apples are tender. Combine powdered sugar and lemon juice; drizzle over pastry while it is warm. Cut into squares and serve either warm or cold.

PUMPKIN PUDDING CAKE

Servings: 10-12

An unusual cake-topped pumpkin pudding that is always a hit.

1 (29 oz.) can unseasoned pumpkin
1 (12 oz.) can evaporated milk
4 eggs, lightly beaten
¾ cup sugar
1 tsp. salt
1 tsp. ground ginger

1 tsp. ground cinnamon
½ tsp. ground cloves
1 (18¼ oz.) pkg. yellow or spice
  cake mix
1 cup chopped nuts
⅔ cup butter or margarine, melted

Mix pumpkin, milk, eggs, sugar, salt, ginger, cinnamon and cloves together. Pour into a lightly buttered 9 x 13 pan. Sprinkle cake mix over the top. Sprinkle with chopped nuts. Pour melted butter over all. Bake at 325° for about 1 hour and 15 minutes or until a tester comes out clean. Cool in pan on a wire rack. Serve warm or cool.

CINNAMON CREAM
WITH CHOCOLATE CRUST

This dessert is simple but elegant, and superb with fresh raspberries.

4 cups crushed chocolate wafer
  crumbs
½ cup butter or margarine, melted
1 tbs. ground cinnamon
4 (2-inch long) cinnamon sticks
4½ cups half and half

2 cups sugar
3 envelopes (3 tbs.) plain gelatin
¾ cup cold water
3 cups sour cream
2 tsp. vanilla

Combine crushed chocolate wafers, butter and cinnamon; press mixture firmly into a buttered 9 x 13 baking dish. Bake at 350° for 15 minutes. Cool.

In a saucepan, combine cinnamon sticks, half and half and sugar. Heat for 10 minutes but do not allow to boil. Soften gelatin in cold water and stir it into hot cream. Cool and chill until mixture begins to thicken.

Remove cinnamon sticks. Beat sour cream and vanilla until smooth and fold them into the cinnamon cream mixture. Spoon into prepared crust, cover and chill 4 to 6 hours until set or overnight. Keep refrigerated until ready to serve. Cut into squares to serve.

LEMON-BUTTERMILK MOLDED DESSERT

The tangy smooth buttermilk cream contrasts nicely with the crunchy granola bottom layer in this unusual dessert, which can be prepared the day before.

4 cups granola, crushed to remove lumps
½ cup butter or margarine, melted
grated peel of 2 lemons
6 envelopes (6 tbs.) plain gelatin
1½ cups cold water

1½ cups sugar
½ tsp. salt
9 cups (1 qt. plus 1 cup) buttermilk
6 tbs. lemon juice
2 tsp. vanilla

Combine granola, butter and lemon peel; press firmly into bottom of a 9 x 13 baking dish. Bake at 350° for 15 minutes. Cool.

In a large saucepan, soak gelatin in cold water until soft. Stir over low heat until dissolved. Remove from heat; add sugar and salt. Add buttermilk, lemon juice and vanilla; stir until well blended.

Pour buttermilk mixture on top of granola crust and chill 4 to 6 hours until set or overnight. Refrigerate until ready to serve. Cut into squares to serve.

NAN'S BANANA SPLIT CAKE

Servings: 10-12

Who doesn't love a banana split? This dessert confection leaves nothing to be desired.

2 cups crushed graham cracker
  crumbs or crushed vanilla wafer
  crumbs
4 tbs. butter or margarine, melted
3 tbs. sugar
1¾ cups powdered sugar
2 eggs
1 cube butter or margarine, softened

1 tsp. vanilla
4 ripe, but firm, bananas
4 tbs. lemon juice
1 (20 oz.) can crushed pineapple,
  drained
1½ cups heavy cream, whipped
1½ cups finely chopped nuts

Combine crumbs, butter and sugar; press into bottom of a 9 x 13 serving dish. With an electric beater, mix powdered sugar, eggs, butter and vanilla until mixture is fluffy, about 10 minutes. Spread on top of crumbs. Slice bananas and toss with lemon juice. Spread crushed pineapple on top of fluffy mixture and top with sliced bananas. Chill at least 4 hours. Just before serving, spread with whipped cream and sprinkle with nuts.

INDEX

SERVE CREATIVE, EASY, NUTRITIOUS MEALS — COLLECT THEM ALL

The Bread Machine Cookbook
The Bread Machine Cookbook #2
The Sandwich Maker Cookbook
The Juicer Book
Bread Baking (traditional), revised
The Kid's Cookbook, revised
The Kid's Microwave Cookbook
15-Minute Meals for 1 or 2
Recipes for the 9x13 Pan
Turkey, the Magic Ingredient
Chocolate Cherry Tortes and Other Lowfat Delights
Lowfat American Favorites
Lowfat International Cuisine
The Hunk Cookbook
Now That's Italian!
Fabulous Fiber Cookery

Low Salt, Low Sugar, Low Fat Desserts
What's for Breakfast?
Healthy Cooking on the Run
Healthy Snacks for Kids
Creative Soups & Salads
Quick & Easy Pasta Recipes
Muffins, Nut Breads and More
The Barbecue Book
The Wok
New Ways with Your Wok
Quiche & Soufflé Cookbook
Easy Microwave Cooking
Compleat American Housewife 1787
Cooking for 1 or 2
Brunch
Cocktails & Hors d'Oeuvres
Meals in Minutes

New Ways to Enjoy Chicken
Favorite Seafood Recipes
No Salt, No Sugar, No Fat Cookbook
The Fresh Vegetable Cookbook
Modern Ice Cream Recipes
Crepes & Omelets
Time-Saving Gourmet Cooking
New International Fondue Cookbook
Extra-Special Crockery Pot Recipes
Favorite Cookie Recipes
Authentic Mexican Cooking
Fisherman's Wharf Cookbook
The Best of Nitty Gritty
The Creative Lunch Box

Write or call for our free catalog.
Bristol Publishing Enterprises, Inc.
P.O. Box 1737, San Leandro, CA 94577
(800)346-4889; in California (510)895-4461